MODERNISM
AND THE
HARLEM
RENAISSANCE

Houston A. Baker, Jr.

The University of Chicago Press
Chicago and London

The University of Chicago Press, Chicago 60637
The University of Chicago Press, Ltd., London

© 1987 by The University of Chicago
All rights reserved. Published 1987
Paperback edition 1989
Printed in the United States of America

98 97 96 95 94   6 5

Library of Congress Cataloging-in-Publication Data

Baker, Houston A.
  Modernism and the Harlem renaissance.

  Bibliogrpahy: p.
  Includes index.
    1. American literature—Afro-American authors—
History and criticism.   2. American literature—
20th century—History and criticism.   3. American
literature—New York (N.Y.)—History and criticism.
4. Harlem Renaissance.   5. Modernism (Literature)—
United States.   6. Afro-Americans in literature.
7. Afro-American arts—New York (N.Y.)   I. Title.
PS153.N5B25   1987   810'.9'896   87-5014

ISBN 0-226-03525-5 (pbk.)

MODERNISM
AND THE
HARLEM
RENAISSANCE

1 7 SEP 2001

In loving (and re-sounding)
memory of my father,
Houston A. Baker, Sr.
1908—1983

emmuselé, hurlant qu'elle était gutturale, ta voix, qui parlait dans le silence des ombres.

Aimé Césaire
"Afrique"

Blackface is the easiest make-up in the entire make-up box, and requires little or no experience to do acceptably. While any other character requires a great deal of thought, study and experimental work, the "nigger" make-up is most elemental, simple in application and anyone using the least care can achieve a satisfactory result, with little or no practice.

Herbert Powell
The World's Best Book of Minstrelsy

Maroon men throughout the hemisphere developed extraordinary skills in guerrilla warfare. To the bewilderment of their European enemies, whose rigid and conventional tactics were learned on the open battlefields of Europe, these highly adaptable and mobile warriors took maximum advantage of local environments, striking and withdrawing with great rapidity, making extensive use of ambushes to catch their adversaries in crossfire, fighting only when and where they chose, depending on reliable intelligence networks among nonmaroons (both slave and white settlers), and often communicating by horns.

Richard Price
Maroon Societies

Harlem is vicious
modernism. BangClash.
Vicious the way its made.
Can you stand such Beauty?
So violent and transforming?

Amiri Baraka
"Return of the Native"

Contents

List of Illustrations
xi

Preface
xiii

Modernism and the Harlem Renaissance
I

Notes
109

Index
117

Illustrations

Title page of Alain Locke's *The New Negro* (1925)   xx

Thomas Dartmouth Rice as Jim Crow   19

Mrs. Stowe's "Topsy"   23

Title page of *Up from Slavery*, first edition   26

Billy Kersands   34

Bert Williams   35

Cover design of Charles Chesnutt's
The Conjure Woman   42

"Let Us Cheer the Weary Traveller"   59

"Of the Training of Black Men"   61

The original Fisk Jubilee Singers   67

A Maroon Warrior   78

The Brown Madonna   80

Alain Locke   88

Gertrude "Ma" Rainey   96

An Afro-American family dwelling, 1940s   97

The author's family   105

Preface

Two signs—"modernism" and "Harlem Renaissance"—coalesce in the following discussion, but not in altogether familiar ways. Traditionally in discussions of Afro-American literature and culture, "modernism" implies the work of British, Irish, and Anglo-American writers and artists of the early twentieth century. The collaged allusiveness of T. S. Eliot's *The Waste Land* and Joyce's *Ulysses,* the cubist reveries of Picasso, the imagism of Pound, or the subversive politics of surrealists—all have been implicit objects or processes for commentators treating modernism and Afro-American literature and culture. I remember a long conversation with a brilliant young black man that carried us from the steps of Connecticut Hall at Yale, to a local cafeteria, to Sterling Library, and then out into the open air again. He was adamant in his claim that *only* Melvin Tolson among the vast panoply of Afro-American writers had become a successfully "modern" writer (before, say, Baldwin or Ellison)—by which he meant that only Tolson, in his view, sounded like Eliot, or Joyce, or Pound, or . . .

Now, I do not want to submit a mere anecdote as evidence that all spokespersons and analysts of Afro-American expressive traditions have shared a single view of "modernism." But I do want to insist that the moment of the 1920s known as the "Harlem Renaissance" has frequently been faulted for its "failure" to produce *vital, original, effective,* or "modern" art in the manner, presumably, of British, Anglo-American, and Irish creative endeavors. To wit, the signal outpouring of black expressive energies during the American 1920s is considered by one of its better-known critics, Nathan Huggins, as "provincial"—a word for which one might substitute, I suppose, "old-fashioned," or even "moribund." The familiar creators of Harlem—Countee Cullen and Claude McKay, Alain Locke and Nella Larsen, Langston Hughes and Jean Toomer—do not, in the opinion of any number of commentators, sound "modern."

My following discussion, therefore, will seem, at least, nontraditional. For I disagree entirely with the general problematic I have just suggested, a problematic that judges the Harlem 1920s a "failure." In my discussion I offer what is perhaps a sui generis definition of *modern Afro-American sound* as a function of a specifically Afro-American discursive practice.

I began pondering issues of modernism and Afro-American expressive culture when I was invited to participate in the Cambridge History of American Literature project under the directorship of Sacvan Bercovitch. My interest continued through a National Endowment for the Humanities Summer Seminar for College Teachers and the coordination of a panel for the English Institute during the summer of 1985. My orientation—as opposed to my "interest"—where these issues are concerned, however, was conditioned by something far more long-standing and perduring than academic engagements.

The orientation of the reflections that follow derives from a family history and, in particular, from reminiscences of the life of my father, Houston A. Baker, Sr., who died in 1983. Reflecting on the labors of generations of black men and women in the United States who have been exploited, segregated, physically and verbally abused, denied access to opportunity, and called all manner of untoward names, and who have, nonetheless, forged a mighty identity and *forced* the white world to stand in awe and, sometimes, to effect powerful imitations of their signal labors—thinking on such indisputable facts of our family history (and on my father as metonym for that history) I suddenly wondered who, precisely, had consigned the Harlem Renaissance to the domain of "failure" and how we, as Afro-American scholars (but more importantly as descendants of a resonant black lineage), could tolerate this consignment.

I knew, to be sure, that my father had not been a failure either in my own eyes or in the eyes of the community he served for seventy-five years as a dedicated disciple of the teachings of Booker T. Washington. Though he earned graduate degrees from Northwestern University (in hospital administration) and the Wharton School, University of Pennsylvania (MBA), he was denied even the barest hint of what the white interior of American "opportunity" might be. He did not go to school, however, to gain access to such interiors, because he knew very well that *there was no access.* Instead, he went to school to master the forms of "standard" educational processes in the West in order to mold himself into what he ultimately became—one of the smartest, most effective, and keenly businesslike black administrators in the United States. (Which, as any black professional who has made his or her way to productive competence in a racist United States knows, means: My father was an *American* hospital administrator and businessperson par excellence.) It occurred to me that anyone who would call my father a failure would have to have in mind some delusory set of evaluative criteria.

I think the principal delusion might be the assumption that there is no *distinctive* set of "family" sounds, standards, and criteria to invoke where Afro-American history and culture are concerned. That is to say, those who might render the judgment of failure would begin with notions of *objects* to be gained, *projects* to be accomplished, and *processes* to be mastered that stand in direct opposition to a resoundingly peculiar family history.   .

Melding personal and cultural-expressive concerns, I would suggest that judgments on Afro-American "modernity" and the "Harlem Renaissance" that begin with notions of British, Anglo-American, and Irish "modernism" as "successful" objects, projects, and processes to be emulated by Afro-Americans are misguided. It seems to me that Africans and Afro-Americans—through conscious and unconscious designs of various Western "modernisms"—have little in common with Joycean or Eliotic projects. Further, it seems to me that the very *histories* that are assumed in the chronologies of British, Anglo-American, and Irish modernisms are radically opposed to any adequate and accurate account of the history of Afro-American modernism, especially the *discursive* history of such modernism.

The following discussion, therefore—after brief attention to Western modernisms (and I am conscious that I have limited my essay by leaving Continental modernism out of account)—moves to a consideration of the traditional critical and interpretive scheme that has surrounded the Harlem Renaissance. After surveying the limitations of this traditional scheme, I suggest that the analysis of discursive strategies that I designate "the mastery of form" and "the deformation of mastery" produces more accurate and culturally enriching interpretations of the *sound* and *soundings* of Afro-American modernism than do traditional methods. Out of personal reflection, then, comes a set of formulations on expressive modernism and the meaning of speaking (or *sounding*) "modern" in Afro-America.

One revision—an important one, I think—occasioned by these formulations was the reversal of an opinion I once delivered on John Blassingame's assertion that turn-of-the-century black autobiographies provided inspiring models for a culture in transition. Professor Blassingame, who always tunes a sensitive ear to black communal sounds, understood far better than I what a book like Washington's *Up from Slavery* meant in the service of Afro-American modernism. I have come some way, however, since delivering my original, negative judgment; I know now that he was unequivocally correct about the importance of our black, turn-of-the-century speaking manuals.

Out of personal reflection, as well, came my sense that

only the success of Western "confinement" (in the sense intended in Michel Foucault's *Madness and Civilization*, i.e., if you are in a madhouse, then you must be mad) had enabled categories such as ART, LITERATURE, CIVILIZATION, and even MODERNISM to dominate the analytical discourse of Afro-Americans, who are assumed by the confining problematic to be without art, literature, civilization, *and* modernism. That is to say, I came to realize that much of what passes for self-consciously "scholarly" effort on the part of black men and women in the United States is often production self-consciously oriented to win approval from those who have a monopoly on definitions of SCHOLARSHIP. "Careerism" is one sign for the black scholar's inclination to preserve the critical vocabulary *and* the assumptions of a dominating culture in his or her analyses of his or her own "dominated" culture. Another term is "conservatism," and still another, I believe, is "fear." All three produce the same result—the enhancement of the dominating society's power. (Of course, I take it for granted that everyone knows careerist strategies serve the comprador beautifully and frequently result in his or her receipt of white critical approval and material reward.)

Finally, however, personal reflection did not forestall my inclination to provide a model of discursive analysis and ample examples of its interpretive method in order to recode the "Harlem Renaissance" as a comprehensible moment in a distinctive, family modernity. The following discussion, however, could not be retitled "Saving the Harlem Renaissance." For I spend little time arguing the merits of individual "artists" jumbled together by causal *histories*, literary and otherwise. "Movements" are not made and parceled out in neat chronological packages; there was no "Harlem Renaissance" (and certainly not a "voguish" one comprised of disparate artists lumped under a single heading) until *after* the event. I think if the following discussion were to be characterized in fittingly black terms, it might be designated in ways known only to the irrepressibly sly as "a family affair." Beginning with a father and entailing resonant responsibilities for the children, the discussion seeks to resound the legacies of blues geographies in the New World. The value of all expressive legacies, according to the scholar Aby Warburg, "depends upon the subjective make-up of the late-born rather than on the objective character of the classical heritage. . . . Every age has the renaissance it deserves."*

H.A.B.

Philadelphia
December 1985

*E. H. Gombrich, *Aby Warburg: An Intellectual Biography* (1970), p. 238.

MODERNISM
AND THE
HARLEM
RENAISSANCE

THE NEW NEGRO
AN INTERPRETATION

EDITED BY ALAIN LOCKE

BOOK
DECORATION
AND
PORTRAITS
BY
WINOLD
REISS

ALBERT AND CHARLES BONI

NEW YORK   1925

Title page of Alain Locke's 1925 anthology, considered a signal document of the Harlem Renaissance.

1

The term "modernism" has something of the character of Keats's cold pastoral.[1] Promising a wealth of meaning, it locks observers into a questing indecision that can end in unctuous chiasmus. Teased out of thought by the term's promise, essayists often conclude with frustratingly vague specifications. Harry Levin's essay "What Was Modernism?" for example, after providing lists, catalogues, and thought problems, concludes with the claim that modernism's distinguishing feature is its attempt to create "a conscience for a scientific age."[2] Modernism's definitive act, according to Levin, traces its ancestry to "Rabelais, at the very dawn of modernity."

Such an analysis can only be characterized as a terribly general claim about scientific mastery and the emergence of the modern. It shifts the burden of definition from "modernism" to "science" without defining either enterprise.

Robert Martin Adams, in an essay bearing the same title as Levin's, offers a key to modernism's teasing semantics. Adams writes:

> Of all the empty and meaningless categories, hardly any is inherently as empty and meaningless as "the modern." Like "youth," it is a self-destroying concept; unlike "youth," it has a million and one potential meanings. Nothing is so dated as yesterday's modern, and nothing, however dated in itself, fails to qualify as "modern" so long as it enjoys the exquisite privilege of having been created yesterday.[3]

Adams implies that bare chronology makes modernists of us all. The latest moment's production—by definition—instantiates "the modern." And unless we arbitrarily terminate modernism's allowable tomorrows, the movement is unending. Moreover, the temporal indeterminacy of the term allows us to select (quite randomly) structural features that we will call distinctively "modern" on the basis of their chronological proximity to us. We can then read these features over past millennia. Like Matthew Arnold in his Oxford inaugural lecture entitled "On the Modern Element in Literature," we can discover what is most distinctively modern in works a thousand years old.

As one reads essay after essay, one becomes convinced that Ihab Hassan's set of provocative questions in a work entitled "POSTmodernISM: A Paracritical Bibliography" are apt and suggestive for understanding the frustrating persistence of "modernism" as a critical sign. Hassan queries:

> When will the Modern Period end?
> Has ever a period waited so long? Renaissance? Baroque? Neo-Classical? Romantic? Victorian?
> When will Modernism cease and what comes thereafter?
> What will the twenty-first century call us? and will its voice come from the same side of our graves?
> Does Modernism stretch merely to stretch out our lives? Or, ductile, does it give a new sense of time? The end of periodization? The slow arrival of simultaneity?
> If change changes ever more rapidly, and the future jolts us now, do men, paradoxically, resist both endings and beginnings?[4]

Certainly it is the case that scholars resist consensus on everything—beginnings, dominant trends, and endings—where modernism is concerned.

Yet for Anglo-American and British traditions of literary and artistic scholarship there is a tenuous agreement that some names and works *must* be included in any putatively comprehensive account of modern writing and art. Further, there seems to be an identifiable pleasure in listing features of art and writing that begin to predominate (by Virginia Woolf's time line) on or about December 1910. The names and techniques of the "modern" that are generally set forth constitute a descriptive catalog resembling a natural philosopher's curiosity cabinet. In such cabinets disparate and seemingly discontinuous objects share space because that is the very function of the cabinet—to house or give order to varied things in what appears a rational, scientific manner. Picasso and Pound, Joyce and Kandinsky, Stravinsky and Klee, Brancusi and H. D. are made to form a series. Collage, primitivism, montage, allusion, "dehumanization," and leitmotivs are forced into the same field. Nietzsche and Marx, Freud and Frazier, Jung and Bergson become dissimilar bedfellows. Such naming rituals have the force of creative works like *Ulysses* and *The Waste Land*. They substitute a myth of unified purpose and intention for definitional certainty. Before succumbing to the myth, however, perhaps we should examine the "change" that according to Woolf's calendar occurred on or about December 1910.

Surely that change is most accurately defined as an acknowledgment of radical uncertainty. Where precisely anyone or anything was located could no longer be charted on old maps of "civilization," nor could even the most microscopic observation tell the exact time and space of day. The very conceptual possibilities of both time and space had been dramatically refigured in the mathematics of Einstein and the physics of Heisenberg. A war of barbaric immensity combined with imperialism, capitalism, and totalitarianism to produce a reaction to human possibilities quite different from Walt Whitman's joyous welcoming of the modern. Whitman in the nineteenth century exulted: "Years of the modern! years of the unperform'd!"

For T. S. Eliot, on or about December 1910, the completed and expected performance of mankind scarcely warranted joy. There was, instead, the "Murmur of maternal lamentation" presaging

> Cracks . . . and bursts in the violet air
> Falling towers
> Jerusalem Athens Alexandria
> Vienna London
> Unreal.[5]

Eliot's speaker, however, is comforted by the certainty that there are millennia of fragments (artistic shrapnel) constituting a *civilization* to be mined, a cultured repertoire to act as a shore against ruins. Fitzgerald's Tom Buchanan in *The Great Gatsby* might therefore be a more honestly self-conscious representation of the threat that some artists whom we call "modern" felt in the face of a new world of science, war, technology, and imperialism. "Civilization's going to pieces," Tom confides to an assembled dinner party at his lavish Long Island estate while drinking a corky (but rather impressive) claret. "I've gotten to be a terrible pessimist about things," he continues.[6]

Now, I don't mean to suggest that Anglo-American, British, and Irish moderns did not address themselves with seriousness and sincerity to a changed condition of humankind. Certainly they did. But they also mightily restricted the province of what constituted the tumbling of the towers, and they remained eternally self-conscious of their own pessimistic "becomings." Tom's pessimism turns out to be entirely bookish. It is predicated upon Stoddard's (which Tom remembers as "Goddard's") racialist murmurings. What really seems under threat are not towers of civilization but rather an assumed supremacy of boorishly racist, indisputably sexist, and unbelievably wealthy Anglo-Saxon males. One means of shoring up one's self under perceived threats of "democratization" and a "rising tide" of color is to resort to elitism—to adopt a style that refuses to represent any *thing* other than the stylist's refusal to represent (what Susan Sontag refers to as an "aesthetics of silence"). Another strategy is to claim that one's artistic presentations and performances are quintessential renderings of the unrepresentable—human subconsciousness, for example, or primitive structural underpinnings of a putatively civilized mankind, or the simultaneity of a space-time continuum. Yet another strategy—a somewhat tawdry and dangerous one—is advocacy and allegiance to authoritarian movements or institutions that promise law and order.

Regardless of their strategies for confronting it, though, it was *change*—a profound shift in what could be taken as unquestionable assumptions about the meaning of human life—that moved those artists whom we call "moderns." And it was only a rare one among them who did not have some formula—some "ism"—for checking a precipitous toppling of man and his towers. Futurism, imagism, impressionism, vorticism, expressionism, cubism—all offered explicit programs for the arts *and* the salvation of humanity. Each in its turn yielded to other formulations of the role of the writer and the task of the artist in a changed and always, ever more rapidly changing world.

Today, we are "postmodern." Rather than *civilization*'s having gone to pieces, it has extended its sway in the form of a narrow and concentrated group of powerbrokers scarcely more charming, humane, or informed than Tom Buchanan. To connect the magnificent achievements, breakthroughs, and experiments of an entire panoply of modern intellectuals with fictive attitudes of a fictive modern man (Fitzgerald's Tom) may seem less than charitable. For even though Tom evades the law, shirks moral responsibility, and still ends up rich and in possession of the fairest Daisy of them all (though he ends, that is to say, as the capitalist triumphant, if not the triumphant romantic hero of the novel), there are still other modes of approach to the works of the moderns.

Lionel Trilling, for example, provides one of the most

charitable scholarly excursions to date. He describes modern literature as "shockingly personal," posing "every question that is forbidden in polite society" and involving readers in intimate interactions that leave them uneasily aware of their personal beings in the world.[7] One scholarly reaction to Trilling's formulations, I'm afraid, is probably like that of the undergraduates whom he churlishly suggests would be "rejected" by the efforts of Yeats and Eliot, Pound and Proust. It is difficult, for example, for an Afro-American student of literature like me—one unconceived in the philosophies of Anglo-American, British, and Irish moderns—to find intimacy either in the moderns' hostility to *civilization* or in their fawning reliance on an array of images and assumptions bequeathed by a *civilization* that, in its prototypical form, is exclusively Western, preeminently bourgeois, and optically white.

Alas, Fitzgerald's priggishly astute Nick has only a limited vocabulary when it comes to a domain of experience that I, as an Afro-American, know well: "As we crossed Blackwell's Island a limousine passed us, driven by a white chauffeur, in which sat three modish negroes, two bucks and a girl. I laughed aloud as the yolks of their eyeballs rolled toward us in haughty rivalry."[8] If only Fitzgerald had placed his "pale well-dressed negro" in the limousine or if Joseph Conrad had allowed his Africans actually to be articulate[9] or if D. H. Lawrence had not suggested through Birkin's reflection on African culture that

> thousands of years ago, that which was imminent in himself must have taken place in these Africans: the goodness, the holiness, the desire for creation and productive happiness must have lapsed, leaving the single impulse for knowledge in one sort, mindless progressive knowledge through the senses, knowledge arrested and ending in the senses, mystic knowledge in disintegration and dissolution, knowledge such as the beetles have, which live purely within the world of corruption and cold dissolution.[10]

6

Or if only O'Neill had bracketed the psycho-surreal final trappings of his Emperor's world and given us the stunning account of colonialism that remains implicit in his quip at the close of his list of dramatis personae: "The action of the play takes place on an island in the West Indies, as yet unself-determined by white marines."[11] If any of these moves had been accomplished, then perhaps I might feel at least some of the intimacy and reverence that Trilling suggests.

But even as I recall a pleasurable spring in New Haven when I enjoyed cracking Joycean codes in order to teach *Ulysses*, I realize that the Irish writer's grand monument is not a work to which I shall return with reverence and charitably discover the type of inquisition that Trilling finds so engaging: "[Modern literature] asks us if we are content with our marriages, with our family lives, with our professional lives, with our friends."[12] I am certain that I shall never place *Ulysses* in a group of texts that I describe, to use Trilling's words, as "spiritual" if not "actually religious." Perhaps the reason I shall not is because the questions Trilling finds—correctly or incorrectly—intimately relevant to his life are descriptive only of a bourgeois, characteristically twentieth-century, white Western mentality. As an Afro-American, a person of African descent in the United States today, I spend a great deal of time reflecting that in the world's largest geographies the question Where will I find water, wood, or food for today? is (and has been for the entirety of this century) the most pressing and urgently posed inquiry.

In "diasporic," "developing," "Third World," "emerging"—or whatever adjective one chooses to signify the non-Western side of Chenweizu's title "The West and the Rest of Us"—nations or territories there is no need to pose, in ironical Audenesque ways, questions such as Are we happy? Are we content? Are we free?[13] Such questions presuppose at least an adequate level of sustenance and a sufficient faith in human behavioral alternatives to enable a self-directed questioning. In other words, without food for thought, all modernist bets are off. Rather than reducing the present essay to a discourse on underdevelopment or invoking a different kind of human being, however, what I want to evoke by emphasizing concerns other than those of "civilization" and its discontents is a discursive constellation that marks a change in Afro-American nature that occurred on or about September 18, 1895. The constellation that I have in mind includes Afro-American literature, music, art, graphic design, and intellectual history. It is *not* confined to a traditionally defined belles lettres or to Literature with a capital and capitalist *L*.

In fact, it is precisely the confinement (in the Foucauldian sense discovered in *Madness and Civilization*) of such bourgeois categories (derivatives of Kantian aesthetics) that the present essay seeks to subvert.[14] Hence there will be few sweeps over familiar geographies of a familiar Harlem Renaissance conceived as an enterprise of limited accomplishment and limited liability—"Harlem Renaissance, Ltd." Instead I shall attempt to offer an account of discursive conditions of possibility for what I define as "renaissancism" in Afro-American expressive culture as a whole. I am thus interested less in *individual* "artists" (as my later discussion of Afro-American formal mastery and Paul Laurence Dunbar will make clear) than in areas of expressive production. It is my engagement with these areas of Afro-American production (intellectual history, music, graphic design, stage presence, oratory, etc.) that provides intimacy and that leads me through a specifically Afro-American modernism to blues geographies that are still in search of substantial analysis— and liberation.

2

The affinity that I feel for Afro-American modernism is not altogether characteristic. Scholars have been far from enthusiastic in their evaluation of the "Harlem Renaissance" of the 1920s—an outpouring of writing, music, and social criticism that included some of the earliest attempts by Afro-American artists and intellectuals to define themselves in "modern" terms. Few scholars would disagree that the Harlem Renaissance marks a readily identifiable "modern" moment in Afro-American intellectual history, but most would concede that the principal question surrounding the Harlem Renaissance has been Why did the renaissance fail?

Scarcely four years after "Black Tuesday," that awful moment which plummeted America into depression, a prominent intellectual and contemporary of the renaissance wrote:

> It is a good thing that [the editor] Dorothy West is doing in instituting a magazine [*Challenge*] through which the voices of younger Negro writers can be heard. The term 'younger Negro writers' connotes a degree of disillusionment and disappointment for those who a decade ago hailed with loud huzzas the dawn of the Negro literary millennium. We expected much; perhaps, too much. I now judge that we ought to be thankful for the half-dozen younger writers who did emerge and make a place for themselves.[15]

James Weldon Johnson's disillusionment that the Harlem Renaissance "failed" finds its counterparts and echoes in the scholarship, polemics, and popular rhetoric of the past half century. An avatar of Johnson's disillusionment, for example, is the scholarly disapprobation of Nathan Huggins's provocative study *Harlem Renaissance* (1971). Huggins charges that the Harlem Renaissance failed because it remained provincial. Its spokespersons unfortunately accepted the province of "race" as a domain in which to forge a New Negro identity. Mired in this ethnic provincialism, writers like Countee Cullen, Claude McKay, Langston Hughes, Alain Locke, and others failed to realize that they did not have to battle for a defining identity in America. They needed only, in Huggins's view, to claim "their *patria,* their nativity" as American citizens.[16] The Harvard historian believes that Afro-Americans are—and have always been—inescapably implicated in the warp and woof of the American fabric. He holds that they are in fact nothing other than Americans whose darker pigmentation has been appropriated as a liberating mask by their lighter-complexioned fellow citizens. Hence Afro-Americans are fundamentally bone of the bone—if not flesh of the flesh—of the American people, and both the intricacies of minstrelsy and the aberrations of the Harlem Renaissance are misguided but deeply revelatory products of the way race relations have stumbled and faltered on the boards of progressivist optimism in the United States.

While Huggins adduces provinciality and narrowness as causes for a failed Harlem Renaissance, his contemporary and fellow Afro-American historian David Levering Lewis takes a contrary view. Lewis ascribes Harlem's failings to a tragically wide, ambitious, and delusional striving on the part of renaissance intellectuals. Writing ten years after Huggins, Lewis describes the appearance of Alain Locke's compendium of creative, critical, and scholarly utterances, *The New Negro* (1925):

 . . . its thirty-four Afro-American contributors (four were white) included almost all the future Harlem Renaissance regulars—an incredibly small band of artists, poets, and writers upon which to base Locke's conviction that the race's "more immediate hope rests in the revaluation by white and black alike of the Negro in terms of his artistic endowments and cultural contributions, past and prospective." To suppose that a few superior people, who would not have filled a Liberty Hall quorum or Ernestine Rose's 135th Street library, were to lead ten million Afro-Americans into an era of opportunity and justice seemed irresponsibly delusional.[17]

Lewis suggests that this delusional vision was a direct function of a rigidly segregated United States. Unlike Huggins, who assumes *patria* as a given, Lewis claims that Afro-Americans turned to art during the twenties precisely because there was no conceivable chance of their assuming *patria*—or anything else in white America. Art seemed to offer the only means of advancement because it was the *only* area in America—from an Afro-American perspective—where the color line had not been rigidly drawn. Excluded from politics and education, from profitable and challenging areas of the professions, and brutalized by all American economic arrangements, Afro-Americans adopted the arts as a domain of hope and an arena of possible progress.

Lewis's stunningly full research reveals the merits of his thesis. He provides a grim look at dire economic and social restrictions that hemmed blacks in everywhere in the United States during the 1920s. Exceptional art—like effective and liberating social strategies—was perhaps a quite illusory Afro-American goal. In the end, all of Harlem's sound and flair could not alter the indubitably American fact that black men and women, regardless of their educational or artistic accomplishments, would always be poorer, more brutally treated, and held in lower esteem than their white American counterparts. The renaissance thus reveals itself in retrospect, according to Lewis, as the product of middle-class black "architects [who] believed in ultimate victory through the maximizing of the exceptional. They [members of the 'talented tenth'] deceived themselves into thinking that race relations in the United States were amenable to the assimilationist patterns of a Latin country."[18]

The gap between the Afro-American masses and the talented tenth could not have been manifested more profoundly than in the latter's quixotic assimilationist assumptions. For, ironically, the most acute symbol of Harlem's surge at the wall of segregation is not poems or interracial dinner parties, according to Lewis, but rather the Harlem riot of 1935, in which thousands took to the streets and unleashed their profound frustrations by destroying millions of dollars worth of white property. The riot, for Lewis, offers the conclusive signal that the strivings of the twenties were delusional and that the renaissance was fated to end with a bang of enraged failure.

Johnson, Huggins, and Lewis are all scholars who merit respect for their willingness to assess an enormously complex array of interactions spanning more than a decade of Afro-American artistic, social, and intellectual history. Thanks to their efforts, we have far more than a bare scholarly beginning when we attempt to define one of the seminal moments of Afro-American "modernism." Yet the scholarly reflections that we possess are, unfortunately, governed by a problematic—a set of questions and issues—that makes certain conclusions and evaluations inevitable. For if one begins with the query that motivates Johnson and others, then one is destined to provide a derogatory account of the twenties. Why did the Harlem Renaissance fail? is the question, and the query is tantamount to the unexpected question sprung by a stranger as one walks a crowded street: "When, Sir, did you stop beating your wife?" Both questions are, of course, conditioned by presuppositions that restrict the field of possible responses. To ask *why* the renaissance failed is to agree, at the very outset, that the twenties did not have profoundly beneficial effects for areas of Afro-American discourse that we have only recently begun to explore in depth. Willing compliance in a problematic of "failure" is equivalent, I believe, to efforts of historians—

black and otherwise—who seek causal explanations for the "failure" of the civil rights movement.

It seems paradoxical that a probing scholar of Lewis's caliber—an investigator who implies strongly that he clearly understands the low esteem in which Afro-Americans will *always* be held—devotes three hundred pages to proving the "failure" of a movement that in the eyes of white America could never have been a success—precisely because it was "Afro-American." The scholarly double bind that forces Afro-Americanists to begin with *given* assessments of black intellectual history and then laboriously work their way to dire conclusions is, quite simply, an unfortunate result of disciplinary control and power politics. The purely hypothetical injunction to an Afro-Americanist from the mainstream might be stated as follows: "Show me, by the best scholarly procedures of the discipline, why the Harlem Renaissance was a failure, and I will reward you. By explaining this *failure,* you will have rendered an 'honest' intellectual service to the discipline, to yourself, and to your race." The primary evaluation where such an injunction is concerned remains, of course, that of the dominating society whose axiological validity and aptitude are guaranteed by its dictation of the governing problematic.

If we return for a moment to Anglo-American and British literary history, it is difficult to conceive of scholars devoting enormous energy to explicating the "failure" of modernism. Surely it is the case that the various "isms" of the first decades of British and American modernism did not forestall wars, feed the poor, cure the sick, empower coal miners in Wales (or West Virginia), or arrest the spread of bureaucratic technology. Furthermore—though apologists will not thank me for saying so—the artistic rebels and rebellions of British and American modernism were often decidedly puerile and undeniably transient. The type of mind set that has governed a Harlem Renaissance problematic would be in force vis-à-vis British and American modernism, I think, if a scholar took Rainer Maria Rilke's evaluation in a letter to a friend as the indisputable truth of modernism's total effect on the world. Writing at the outbreak of World War I, Rilke laments "that such confusion, not-knowing-which-way-to-turn, the whole sad man-made complication of this provoked fate, that exactly this incurably bad condition of things was necessary to force out evidences of whole-hearted courage, devotion and bigness? While we, the arts, the theater, called nothing forth in these very same people, brought nothing to rise and flower, were unable to change anyone."[19] A too optimistic faith in the potential of art may in fact be as signal a mark of British and American modernism's "failure" as of the Harlem Renaissance. I suspect, however, that no group of British or white American scholars would take *failure* as their watchword and governing sign for an entire generation and its products. The predictable corollary of my suspicion is my belief that a new problematic is in order for the Harlem Renaissance. I believe that we must reconceptualize the questions we will ask in order to locate the efforts of the 1920s in a framework that can be called the "changing same" of black American expression.

3

The "changing same" is Amiri Baraka's designation for the interplay between tradition and the individual talent in Afro-American music.[20] Invoked in reference to the Harlem Renaissance and Afro-American modernism, the phrase captures strategies that I designate as *the mastery of form* and *the deformation of mastery*. Such strategies come most decisively to the foreground of black intellectual history with the emergence of Booker T. Washington as a black man who possessed (in his own words) "a reputation that in a sense might be called National."[21] The event that produced this reputation occurred at the moment I postulated earlier as the commencement of Afro-American modernism— September 18, 1895. The event, which lasted just ten minutes, was Washington's delivery of the opening address at the Negro exhibit of the Atlanta Cotton States and International Exposition. I designate Washington's speech as the point at which an agreed upon (by those whites in power, or by those empowered by whites in power) direction was set for a mass of black citizens who had struggled through the thirty years since emancipation buffeted on all sides by strategies, plans, hopes, and movements, organized by any number of popular, or local, black spokespersons, without before 1895 having found an overriding pattern of *national* leadership or an approved plan of action that could guarantee at least the industrial education of a considerable sector of the black populace.

The immensity of the Tuskegee orator's ability (quite cannily won) to take the stage at Atlanta and speak into existence a program, policy, and platform that offered guiding premises and discursive strategies has been remarked by many. But the specifics of his captivating power before a turn-of-the-century audience have not, I think, been fully appreciated. His most influential set of public utterances is contained in *Up from Slavery* (1901), his autobiography and a work that dramatically portrays patterns that I call the mastery of form. Before considering the autobiography's discursive strategies, however, a definition is in order.

When I use the word "form," I do not want to invoke a distinction between form and content and spring the metaphysical trap privileging a primary order of form as an abiding and stabilizing *presence*. For me, "form" has the force of a designated space—presumably, that between traditionally formulated dichotomies such as self and other. A substitute for the term might be *ellipsis,* or *trope,* or *poetic image.* What I have in mind is not a single, easily identifiable structure, or even an easily described spatial apperception.

Form, by any definition accurately available in a world of particle physics and electron microscopy, cannot be taken as the concrete shape of, say, molecules in their solid state. Rather, the very spatial configurations that occur to human observers are selective filterings, results of the "smoothing" or discounting of the heat motion of molecules that our best theories provide. When the cubes of ice intended for a refreshing lemonade (or a more severe potable against academic malaise) melt while we are explaining to a student who has telephoned that his or her "C" is only a letter, a convenient "form" explaining nothing deeply relevant about his or her psyche, we grasp a notion of the arbitrariness of form. "Form" under the impress of *uncertainty* is irreducible to a homunculus, a key "deep-structural" transformation, or a replica. As we move beyond a solid state (such as the ice cubes), our instrumental powers of observation lead not to "primary" forms but to *events*—motions of hypothetical particles unmeasurable.

For the present, I shall use the term "form" to signal a symbolizing fluidity. I intend by the term a family of concepts or a momentary and changing same array of images, figures, assumptions, and presuppositions that a group of people (even one as extensive and populous as a nation) holds to be a valued repository of spirit. And the form most apt for carrying forward such notions is a *mask*.[22]

It is difficult to convey notions of *form* and *mask* in the exact ways that I would like, for the mask as form does not exist as a static object. Rather it takes effect as a center for ritual and can only be defined—like form—from the perspective of action, *motion seen* rather than "thing" observed. I shall make an attempt to convey the notion of mask as form, however, by summoning a familiar imagistic array, a long-standing group of concepts and assumptions that serves as a spiritual repository for a quintessential American ritual. The form, array, mask that I have in mind is the *minstrel mask*. That mask is a space of habitation not only for repressed spirits of sexuality, ludic play, id satisfaction, castration anxiety, and a mirror stage of development, but also for that deep-seated denial of the indisputable humanity of inhabitants of and descendants from the continent of Africa. And it is, first and foremost, the mastery of the minstrel mask by blacks that constitutes a primary move in Afro-American discursive modernism.

The spirit of denial in the minstrel mask is nowhere more defining of a national spirit than in the United States. The mask, for generations on end, has been so persuasively captivating, so effectively engaging in its seeming authenticity, that an astute intellectual like Constance Rourke can actually take it as an adequate and accurate sign of a "tradition" of "Negro literature" predating the "cult" of Afro-American expressivity she found so wearying in the 1940s.

But if Rourke seems too credulous about the authenticity of representations of Afro-America that took place behind the minstrel mask, she is nonetheless capable of a fine analytic dissection when she allows herself to be subjected to what one might call the *sound* emanating from the mask. She records her reaction as follows:

> Early blackface minstrelsy revealed indeed the natural ap-
> propriations of the Negro from the life about him: but
> the persistent stress was primitive, the effect exotic and
> strange with the swaying figures and black faces of the
> minstrels lighted by guttering gas flames or candlelight
> on small country stages or even in the larger theaters.
> Within this large and various pattern lay a fresh context
> of comedy, plain in the intricate, grotesque dancing as
> the minstrels "walked jaw-bone" or accomplished the
> deep complications of the "dubble trubble" or the
> "grapevine twist." A bold comic quality appeared which
> had not developed elsewhere in American humor, that of
> nonsense. With all his comic wild excesses the back-
> woodsman never overflowed into pure nonsense; the
> Yankee did not display it. Perhaps the Negro did not in-
> vent the nonsensical narratives told in song on the min-
> strel stage, but the touch is akin to that of Negro fables in
> song; and nonsense in minstrelsy shows a sharp distinc-
> tion from other humor of the day.

> A little old man was ridin' by,
> His horse was tryin' to kick a fly,
> He lifted his leg towards de south
> An' sent it bang in its own mouth—

> . . . . .

> The note of triumph, dominant in all early American
> humor, appeared in these reflected creations of the
> Negro, but not as triumph over circumstance. Rather
> this was an unreasonably headlong triumph launching
> into the realm of the preposterous.[23]

What Rourke compresses into the space of this lengthy quotation is the psychodrama of the minstrel mask.

If the inhabiting spirit of the mask is, as Rourke suggests, one of nonsense, misappropriation, or mis-hearing (a misconstrual fundamental to American minstrelsy), then the results are as bizarre (and, surely, as appealing) as witch burning or lynching, to suggest other embedding American rituals. The Afro-American writer William Melvin Kelley brilliantly conflates the motions of the minstrel show's ritual with lynching and exorcism in his novel *A Different Drummer* (1962). Threatened with lynching by a southern mob

JIM CROW.

NEW YORK.

Thomas Dartmouth Rice in his representation of Jim Crow. Rice, a white man, is held to have learned the steps of "jumpin' Jim Crow" from a black slave. He was one of the most successful of all minstrel performers during the 1830s and 1840s. (Courtesy of the Chicago Historical Society.)

that is enraged because the Negroes of the region have followed an exodus led by Tucker Caliban (O, happily named protagonist!), Kelley's Reverend Bradshaw is suddenly identified as "our last nigger" by one of the mob. Having made this identification, the group decides that before they kill Bradshaw, they should present him—in a bizarre and archetypally American reversal of the *prisoner's* last wish—with a final request: "Do you know 'Curley-Headed Picaninny Boy'?" they ask. Bradshaw nods, and the narrator comments:

> Of course he knew, everybody knew it; it was a song liberal-minded third-grade music teachers in New York, Chicago, Des Moines, San Francisco, and all the towns in between had their pupils sing to acquaint them with Negro culture; in Cambridge it was sung whenever anyone with a guitar who prided himself as a folk singer got together with a group of people who considered themselves folklorists; it was known all over the country, had been sung for a long time. And Dewey [the youthful Harvardian of Kelley's tale] realized that Bradshaw's nod had signified a knowledge of something else; he knew now and could understand why the Negroes had left without waiting or needing any organizations or leadership.[24]

The whites are enraged when Bradshaw, a Harvard alumnus, sings the song with a British accent and proves inept at minstrel dancing. "You stink!" they exclaim, and drag him off to die.

Combining Kelley's and Rourke's figurations of minstrelsy results not only in a sense of the absurdity implicit in the mask, but also in a notion of minstrelsy's prevalence. To be a *Negro*, the mask mandates, to be a *Negro* one must meld with minstrelsy's contours. (And what a reversal the black entertainers Bert Williams and George Walker effected when they advertised themselves as "Two *real* Coons.") Such a concurrence casts one headlong into the realm of nonsense. The minstrel mask is a governing object in a ritual of *non-sense*. The brand of non-sense to which minstrelsy gives force is best described, I think, by Susan Stewart's observations on "ready-made systems" of nonsense. She writes:

> At times nonsense will effect a traversal that depends upon the availability of a given, or ready-made, system from common sense. The common-sense system provides the closed form within which nonsense effects its rearrangements or substitution of elements. One such use of the play of rearrangement within closed fields is the mnemonic device. Here a structure is used to incorporate all the elements of what is desired to be remembered. For example, there is the mnemonic for the colors of the rainbow (red, orange, yellow, green, blue, indigo, and violet), "Roy G. Biv," which appears in *Ulysses,* and another mnemonic for the same elements, "Read Over Your Greek Books in Vacation." The mnemonic is knowledge centered in itself; it has no meaning outside of its use. It is purely "a device," for it does not "count" on its own.[25]

By misappropriating elements from everyday black use, from the vernacular—the commonplace and commonly sensible in Afro-American life—and fashioning them into a comic array, a mask of *selective* memory, white America fashioned a *device* that only "counts" in relationship to the Afro-American systems of sense from which it is appropriated. The intensity of the minstrel ritual, its frantic replaying to packed and jovial houses, is a function of the "real" Afro-Americans just beyond the theater's doors, beyond the guttering lights of the mind's eye. The device is designed to remind white consciousness that black men and women are *mis-speakers* bereft of humanity—carefree devils strumming and humming all day—unless, in a gaslight misidentification, they are violent devils fit for lynching, a final exorcism that will leave whites alone. Which all returns us to the "mastery of form." For it was in fact the minstrel mask as mnemonic ritual object that constituted the *form* that any Afro-American who desired to be articulate—to speak at all—had to master during the age of Booker T. Washington.

I have suggested that the *sound* emanating from the mask reverberates through a white American discursive universe as the sound of the Negro. If it is true that myth is the detritus of ritual, then the most clearly identifiable atavistic remains of minstrelsy are narratives or stories of ignorant and pathetically comic brutes who speak nonsense syllables. Listen to what minstrelsy made of blacks' understanding of "America." The passage is drawn from a popular minstrel show oration.

> When in de course ob inhuman events it becomes necessary fo' a man to elimnate de constructive difference from de planetary problem, what objective dissolution am de ebberlastin' screech ob a lonesomen Thomas cat got ter do wiv de brickbat flung at him? Dat's so an' more so.

If we turn to a white literary canon, we find Hugh Henry Brackenridge's Cuff in *Modern Chivalry* (1792) constructed to sound as follows: "Massa shentiman; I be cash crab in de Wye river; found ting in de mud; tone, big a man's foot: hole like to he; fetch Massa: Massa say, it be de Indian Mocasson.—Oh! fat de call it all tone."[26] This is *white dada* at its most obscene. The "black" syllables roll on through James Fenimore Cooper's mindless servants and Negro players in *Satanstoe*. They echo in the phonics of *Uncle Tom's Cabin* in such absurd utterances as those that Stowe ascribes to an "old negress." An elderly black woman responds to a classless white scoundrel's injury as follows: "La sakes! jist hear the poor crittur. He's got a mammy, now . . . I can't help kinder pityin' on him."[27] Stowe's treatment of the *younger* Negro woman produces only a distressed wonder:

Mrs. Stowe's exotic creation "Topsy," a character who entered the American popular imagination not only through the novel *Uncle Tom's Cabin* but also through the hundreds of performances of "Tom Shows" derived from the novel, which played relentlessly in the United States and in Europe. (Courtesy of the Museum of the City of New York.)

"Here, Topsy," he added, giving a whistle, as a man would to call the attention of a dog, "give us a song, now, and show us some of your dancing."

The black, glassy eyes glittered with a kind of wicked drollery, and the thing struck up, in a clear shrill voice, an old negro melody, to which she kept time with her hands and feet, spinning round, clapping her hands, knocking her knees together, in a wild, fantastic sort of time, and *producing in her throat all those odd gutteral sounds which distinguish the native music of her race;* and finally, turning a somerset or two, and giving a prolonged closing note, *as odd and unearthly as that of a stream-whistle,* she came suddenly down on the carpet. [my emphasis][28]

The equation of Topsy with a machine in slavery's garden is perhaps the only rhetorically redeeming aspect of this passage. If one were to summon the syllabic idiocies of white plantation novels and add them to what Mark Twain describes in *Pudd'nhead Wilson* as the "base" dialect of the quarters, a dialect he bestows on Jim in *Huckleberry Finn* and on Jim's brutish avatar in *Pudd'nhead,* one would have an array of misspellings, mispronounciations, and misidentifications suitable to span the globe. These sounds are implicit in the haughty eyeball-rollers of *Gatsby* and gather strength in the murmurings of Faulkner's Clytie and Dilsey. They are ritually renewed by Amos and Andy and appear today with mythic and mnemonic force in television's Mr. T, George Jefferson, and tiny Arnold. Obviously, an Afro-American spokesperson who wished to engage in a masterful and empowering play within the minstrel spirit house needed the uncanny ability to manipulate bizarre phonic legacies. For he or she had the task of transforming the mask and its sounds into negotiable discursive currency. In effect, the task was the production of a manual of black speaking, a book of speaking *back and black.*

4

Thirty-two* years after the Emancipation Proclamation, Booker T. Washington changed the minstrel joke by stepping inside the white world's nonsense syllables with oratorical mastery. *Up from Slavery* offers a record and representation of Afro-America's mastery of form. Early in the text we discover that Washington understands the constraints that define Afro-American *sound:*

> As the great day [of emancipation] drew nearer, there was more singing in the slave quarters than usual. It was bolder, had more ring, and lasted later into the night. Most of the verses of the plantation songs had some reference to freedom. True, they had sung those same verses before, but they had been careful to explain that the "freedom" in these songs referred to the next world, and had no connection with life in this world. Now they gradually *threw off the mask;* and were not afraid to let it be known that the "freedom" in their songs meant freedom of the body in this world. [P. 39, my emphasis]

Playing *behind* a pious mask is as central to the narrator's characterization of black quarters as the renaming that he describes: "In some way a feeling got among the coloured people that it was far from proper for them to bear the surname of their former owners, and a great many of them took other surnames" (p. 41).

A liberating manipulation of masks and a revolutionary *renaming* are not features commonly ascribed to the efforts of Booker T. Washington. Yet the narrator's clear awareness

UP FROM SLAVERY

AN AUTOBIOGRAPHY

BY

BOOKER T. WASHINGTON

AUTHOR OF "THE FUTURE OF THE AMERICAN NEGRO"

NEW YORK

DOUBLEDAY, PAGE & CO.

1901

Title page of *Up from Slavery,* first edition.

of the importance of such strategies appears at the very opening of *Up from Slavery*. What causes one to bracket (in an almost phenomenological manner) such liberating strategies is the way the narrator keeps culturally specific information hushed to a low register beneath his clamorous workings of the minstrel tradition.

His working of minstrelsy's nonsensical stereotypes begins, most outrageously, when he recalls his mother: "One of my earliest recollections is that of my mother cooking a chicken late at night, and awakening her children for the purpose of feeding them. How or where she got it I do not know. I presume, however, it was procured from our owner's farm" (p. 31). *Up from Slavery* is barely begun. We are two pages into the narrative when we are confronted by a "chicken-stealing darky"—as mother. How soothing and reassuring such a formidably familiar image of "Negro behavior" must have been to Washington's white readers! Such portraiture was bound to overshadow the type of epic discourse that marks a subsequent observation such as this one:

> This experience of a whole race beginning to go to school for the first time [during Reconstruction], presents one of the most interesting studies that has ever occurred in connection with the development of any race. Few people who were not right in the midst of the scenes can form any exact idea of the intense desire which the people of my race showed for an education. *As I have stated*, it was a whole race trying to to go school. Few were too young, and none too old, to make the attempt to learn. [P. 44, my emphasis]

The repeated announcement of the subject in the passage, pre-fixed by the phrase "as I have stated," comes so hard upon the opening epic intentions that it appears the narrator *knows* that no one in his white audience will listen to sounds of an epic. In order to ensure attention, therefore, he must employ strategies such as repetition—or the summoning to the stage of comic, unprepared, and grossly pitiable darkies.

"Bring up the shines, gentlemen! Bring up the little shines!" is the way Ellison's school superintendent in *Invisible Man* captures the necessities of Washington's situation.[29] And, indeed, the following lines from *Up from Slavery* come like a kick in the stomach and stand in blatant contrast to the epic note already introduced:

> It could not have been expected that a people who had spent generations in slavery, and before that generations in the darkest heathenism, could at first form any proper conception of what an education meant. . . . The ambition to secure an education was most praiseworthy and encouraging. The idea, however, was too prevalent that, as soon as one secured a little education, in some unexplainable way he would be free from most of the hardships of the world, and, at any rate, could live without manual labor. [P. 71]

One of the utterly extraordinary things about this passage is the way it revises the tone characterizing a first epic view of blacks turning toward education at the dawn of freedom. The invocations of "heathenism" and "slavery" become comprehensible, however, when one realizes that the passage appears in a chapter entitled "Reconstruction."

Any southern spokesperson—and this was, *preeminently,* the role that Washington occupied—who would be kindly received by a southern audience at the turn of the century had to set forth a dim view of black Reconstruction politics. Washington's narrator not only plays the role of a judiciously southern, post-Reconstruction racist but also supplies a preposterous character direct from minstrelsy to play the darky role in this condemnatory drama:

> I remember there came into our neighbourhood one of this class [Negro teachers who could do little more than write their names], who was in search of a school to teach, and the question arose while he was there as to the shape of the earth and how he would teach the children concerning this subject. He explained his position in the matter by saying that he was prepared to each that the earth was either flat or round, according to the preference of a majority of his patrons. [P. 72]

The continuation of such "darky jokes"—of what I call *sounds* of the minstrel mask—flows from the mother as chicken thief (our origins in "jes some sich mis'chief, boss") through a condemnation and mockery of Afro-American professionals in the chapter on Reconstruction. In its drama of condemnation, this chapter also presents a deceived body of Afro-Americans who reside in the nation's capital and have been victimized by their removal from southern "country districts." These urbanites have suffered the false guidance of higher education, yielding to wastefulness and sin. "I saw," says the narrator, "young coloured men who were not earning more than four dollars a week spend two dollars or more for a buggy on Sunday to ride up and down Pennsylvania Avenue in order that they might try to convince the world that they were worth thousands" (p. 76). In harmony with white Northern sentiment, the narrator wishes that "by some power of magic . . . [he could] remove the great bulk of these people into the country districts [of the South] and plant them upon the soil, upon the solid and never deceptive foundation of Mother Nature, where all nations and races that have ever succeeded have gotten their start,—a start that at first may be slow and toilsome, but one that nevertheless is real" (p. 77).

Epic gives way to pastoral; a black *nation* is displaced by a deceived urban sector in need of redemption. Implicit in the drama of condemnation is the real theme of the piece: the aspirations that characterized a *federal* period of Reconstruction (metonymically signaled by the District of Columbia) must be relinquished. More realistic goals are necessary to meet incumbencies of a new *regional* (the New South) era in which blacks will cast down their buckets where they are and seek advice and counsel from southern whites.

The narrator plays out this discursive drama in ways clearly identifiable as masterful *strategies of attraction*. His cullings from a bizarre white assemblage of distorted syllables gathers force and frequency as he moves beyond Reconstruction. There is, for example, his presentation of the ignorantly comic darky whose political sagacity is recorded as follows:

> "We wants you to be sure to vote jes' like we votes. We can't read de newspapers very much, but we knows how to vote, an' we wants you to vote jes' like we votes. . . . We watches de white man, and we keeps watching de white man till we finds out which way de white man's gwine to vote; an' when we finds out which way de white man's gwine to vote, den we votes 'xactly de other way. Den we know we's right." [P. 88]

Surely this is a voice heard only in the theater of minstrel madness, just as the inhabitants of the "country districts" that Washington presents are grievous caricatures. Witness the man whose help he solicits to renovate a henhouse: "When I told . . . [the] old coloured man who lived near, and who sometimes helped me, that our school had grown so large that it would be necessary for us to use the henhouse for school purposes, and that I wanted him to help me give it a thorough cleaning out the next day, he replied, in the most earnest manner: 'What you mean, boss? You sholy ain't gwine clean out de hen-house in de *day*-time?'" (p. 98). The old man is surely akin to the pathetic old "An'ty" who hobbles into a room at Tuskegee and, despite her obvious poverty, offers Washington six eggs: "'Mr. Washin'ton, God knows I spent de bes' days of my life in slavery. . . . I ain't got no money, but I wants you to take dese six eggs, what I been savin' up, and I wants you to put dese six eggs into de eddication of dese boys an' gals'" (p. 99).

There are other examples in Washington's autobiography of the narrator's self-conscious adoption of minstrel tones and types to keep his audience tuned in. These tones and types, as I have suggested, are reassuring *sounds* from the black quarters. Although the narrator may be stunningly capable of standard English phraseology, crafty political analyses, and smooth verbal gymnastics that move him through an amazing invocation and half-invention of a pastoral Eden at Tuskegee (replete with the founder and his wife figured as a godlike Moses and a tireless helpmate Eve), there can be no worry that the Negro is getting "out of hand." For at all the proper turns, there are comforting sounds and figures of a minstrel theater that we know so well—"Look away! Look away! Look Away! Dixie Land."

Given that *Up from Slavery* has sometimes been considered merely an imitative version of Horatio Alger or of Andrew Carnegie's *Gospel of Wealth* (1889), how can one justify an emphasis on self-conscious design—on a culturally specific and canny rhetorical appropriation that I call the mastery of form? One possible answer to this question can be formulated in structural terms. In Washington's work more than forty of two hundred total pages are devoted to oratorical concerns. In chapters entitled "Two Thousand Miles for a Five-minute Speech," "The Atlanta Exposition Address," and "The Secrets of Success in Public Speaking," Washington's work becomes a *how-to* manual, setting forth strategies of address (ways of talking black and back) designed for Afro-American empowerment. The narrator provides one explanation for his success as a public speaker:

> If in an audience of a thousand people there is one person who is not in sympathy with my views, or is inclined to be doubtful, cold, or critical, I can pick him out. When I have found him I usually go straight at him, and it is a great satisfaction to watch the process of his thawing out. I find that the most effective medicine for such individuals is administered at first in the form of a story, although I never tell an anecdote simply for the sake of telling one. [P. 161]

Surely Washington's narrator—a man who describes his life as unrelieved work and who is more enamored of biography and fact than of fiction and games—never tells a story "simply for the sake of telling one." No, his mind is undoubtedly always fixed on some intended gain, on a *mastery* of stories and their telling that leads to Afro-American advancement. The most scandalous instance of his deeply intentional play on minstrel form is coextensive with patterns set in motion early in the narrative. It occurs in fact in the Atlanta Exposition Address—an address transcribed in the autobiography as an embedded document.

A white farmer tells Washington on the day before his Atlanta talk that he will have to please an audience composed of white northerners, white southerners, and blacks. "I am afraid," says the farmer, "that you have got yourself into a tight place" (p. 144). But Washington's speech is an overwhelming success with black and white alike. It includes tributes to northern philanthropy, gratitude to southern patriarchs, and prescriptions for Afro-American accommodation in an age of Jim Crow. It also includes the *sound* of minstrelsy. Listen:

> Starting thirty years ago with ownership here and there in a few quilts and pumpkins and *chickens (gathered from miscellaneous sources)* . . . [P. 149]

SCANDAL is the only designation for the appearance of such a *sound* (a chicken-thieving tonality) in the first address presented in the South by a black man considered a *national* leader. Extricating himself from a "tight place" and finding room for an authentic voice seem to occasion the scandalous for an Afro-American speaker.

Rather than going straight at a possibly somnolent white southern audience in Atlanta—and at lovers of minstrelsy throughout the nation—Washington strikes a "straight lick with a crooked stick." He turns minstrel nonsense into what he believes is the only available good sense, or, sense intended for a common black good. The efficaciousness of his "public speaking" is captured in another of the embedded documents in *Up from Slavery*. "I will be very glad," reads the document, "to pay the bills for the library building as they are incurred, to the extent of twenty thousand dollars, and I am glad of this opportunity to show the interest that I have in your noble work." The letter is signed "Andrew Carnegie." Further evidence of the success of *Up from Slavery's* rhetorical mastery is offered by the changed status of Tuskegee revealed at the close of the work. Commencing in a stable and a henhouse, the school is transformed during the course of the narrative into a handsomely endowed and architecturally attractive oasis of skills and morality in the midst of southern "country districts." One implicit lesson of Washington's narrative, therefore, is that public speaking—indeed, the Afro-American's ability to find a voice at all—is a function of the mastery of form. Like Billy Kersands stretching the minstrel face to a successful black excess, or Bert Williams and George Walker converting nonsense sounds and awkwardly demeaning minstrel steps into pure kinesthetics and masterful black artistry, so Washington takes up types and tones of nonsense to earn a national reputation and its corollary benefits for the Afro-American masses.[30] He demonstrates in his manipulations of form that there *are* rhetorical possibilities for crafting a voice out of tight places. What, then, of chicken stealing and the mother? The narrator continues his earlier report with these words:

> Some people may call this [my mother's action] theft. If such a thing were to happen now, I should condemn it as theft myself. But taking place at the time it did, and for the reason that it did, no one could make me believe that my mother was guilty of thieving. She was simply a victim of the system of slavery. [P. 31]

It seems we must conceive Washington's appropriation of the minstrel image (so intimately linked with the mother and so casuistically explained) as theft. It is in fact a Promethean cultural appropriation, since he surely took images that fueled the minstrel theater and used them to draw attention to the contours, necessities, and required programs

NEW EPOCH IN NEGRO MINSTRELSY

UNDER THE MANAGEMENT OF R. VOELCKER

America's Oldest Minstrel

KERSANDS

Under Spacious Canvas

The Famous and Original

"BILLY"

The Minstrel King

MINSTRELS

Home Office:
Times Building

Billy Kersands, one of the most talented of Afro-American minstrel performers.

Bert Williams, the grand master of Afro-American minstrels, who made his way to the Ziegfeld Follies. (Courtesy of Milton Meltzer.)

of his own culture. The mother's act thus offers instruction in (and nourishes) a cultural voice won from slavery's victimization and silencing. And *Up from Slavery* as a whole projects a model for the mastery of form that serves as type and figuration for the Afro-American spokesperson. In his provision of the model, Washington—offspring and descendant of slavery's misappropriations—achieves an effective modernity. His "speaking manual" is a sign and a wonder. It emerges from a mass of southern black folk who sought ways beyond factionalism, uncertainty, oppression, and minstrel nonsense that marred their lives during thirty uneasy years from emancipation to the dawn of a new century.

5

To designate Washington rather than, say, Paul Laurence Dunbar as the quintessential herald of modernism in black expressive culture is not willful revisionism. For I am interested in a definition of the mastery of form that renders it more than a strategy adopted for the aesthetic satisfaction of the individual artist. Indeed, I am interested in the strategy to precisely the extent that it ensures cognitive exploration and affective transformations leading to the growth and *survival* of a nation. Washington is "modern" in my view, then, because he earnestly projected the flourishing of a southern, black Eden at Tuskegee—a New World garden to nurture hands, heads, and hearts of a younger generation of agrarian black folk in the "country districts."

The Tuskegean was, as his contemporary Afro-American spokesperson Charles Chesnutt pointed out to a querulous W. E. B. DuBois, an inhabitant in and a worker for the black south. In 1910, DuBois protested—among other statements made by Washington that year in England—the assertion that "any one who lives in the South, where the black men are so numerous, knows that the situation, so far from becoming more difficult or dangerous, becomes more and more reassuring."[31] Chesnutt responded shrewdly to DuBois's resentment:

> This [claim] is a matter of opinion, and Mr. Washington lives in the South, while not more than one or two of the signers of the protest [drafted by you] do, unless Washington [D.C.] be regarded as part of the South. Person-

ally, I have not been any farther South than Washington
but once in twenty-seven years. [P. 241]

(Is it possible that in defending Washington, who was a
close friend of his family, Chesnutt is signifying on DuBois
by repeating the *true* southerner's name three times in two
sentences?) The point is well made. Washington had a regional (some would say *sectional*, or even *peculiar*) authority
in matters black and southern. His avowed goal was to train
the Afro-American masses in a way that would ensure their
inestimable value to a white world—that would, in a word,
enable them to survive.

Now Paul Laurence Dunbar, who was Washington's
contemporary and a spokesperson generally identified as the
first Afro-American poet of "artistic" distinction, is never a
southerner in the sense that the Tuskegeean is. His place of
residence is Ohio, and the land of his heart's desire is American artistic recognition for his individual ability to write
standard English poetry. (One imaginatively hears the quiet
Kafkaesque moan, "I wanted them to admire my fasting.")
Dunbar thus comes to the mastery of form with the chafing
resentment of a romantic adolescent. To wit:

> He sang of love when earth was young,
> And Love, itself, was in his lays.
> But ah, the world, it turned to praise
> A jingle in a broken tongue.[32]

Dunbar lamented to his good friend James Weldon Johnson,
"I've got to write dialect poetry; it's the only way I can
get them to listen to me."[33] Johnson's characterization of
his admired friend and sometimes collaborator in the early
New York black theatricals seems apt. He writes in his preface to *The Book of American Negro Poetry* that "in his actions
[Dunbar] was impulsive as a child, sometimes even erratic;
indeed, his intimate friends almost looked upon him as a
spoiled boy."[34]

It is true that Dunbar offered the example par excellence of a tragic hemming in of Afro-American *artistic* aspiration. And none can deny his skill in recording the anguish of constraint in the slow, somber rhythms of a poem that, in part, justifies the invocation of "the mask" as an appropriate trope for turn-of-the-century Afro-American discourse. His poem "We Wear the Mask" is a landmark of black expressivity.

> We wear the mask that grins and lies,
> It hides our cheeks and shades our eyes,—
> This debt we pay to human guile;
> With torn and bleeding hearts we smile,
> And mouth with myriad subtleties.
>
> Why should the world be overwise,
> In counting all our tears and sighs?
> Nay, let them only see us, while
> We wear the mask.
>
> We smile, but, O great Christ, our cries
> To thee from tortured souls arise.
> We sing, but oh the clay is vile
> Beneath our feet, and long the mile;
> But let the world dream otherwise,
> We wear the mask! [P. 71]

The poem rolls through solemn, Christian meters with the breast-forward stoicism of William Ernest Henley's *Invictus:* "In the fell clutch of circumstance / I have not winced nor cried aloud." Rather than recognize that the black soul's eternal indebtedness is a result of *white* guile, the speaker *accepts* an indebtedness to "guile" as a force—not unlike a cosmic spirit making life bearable—that enables stoicism. In other words, it is as though Dunbar's speaker plays the masking game without an awareness of its status as a game. It seems that he does not adopt masking as self-conscious gamesmanship in opposition to the game white America has run on him. And he surely does not have as one of his goals the general progress of the Afro-American populace.

Rather, he assumes disguise as a holy martyr, as one whose colossal talent (yes, even his messianic potential) has been dwarfed by circumstance. The world's ignorance of his suffering (his exquisitely artistic "fasting") is fuel for fires of self-aggrandizement: possibly, the "world" (meaning white critics of reputation) will fail to see the grandeur of the poetic action resonant in even the poem "We Wear the Mask." Alas!

I do not want to invalidate the pain of Dunbar's tragically brief career. I do want to suggest, though, that the attitude and *sound* of Dunbar's poem are vastly different from that implicit in the following assertion from *Up from Slavery:*

> When a white boy [yes, the lexical item "boy" is, in fact, Washington's] undertakes a task, it is taken for granted that he will succeed. On the other hand, people are usually surprised if the Negro boy does not fail. In a word, the Negro youth starts out with the presumption against him. [P. 48]

(It would seem the Tuskegeean understood the "game" implicit in a "problematic of failure" long before our era.) Washington knows the *game*. And someone as proximate to the abhorrences of slavery as Dunbar—whose father was a fugitive and whose mother recounted stories of slavery to her young son—should know it too. Anyone with Dunbar's background who did not realize the guile and game of minstrelsy for what they were, who could in fact whine that the most powerful literary critic of his era had done him "harm" by praising and ensuring the publication and sale of his dialect poetry—any black writer of this stamp had to be naive, politically innocent, or simply "spoiled."

By contrast, what one sees in Washington's discourse is the *nod*—not unlike that of Kelley's fictive Bradshaw. When white folks ask if he can, in the words of one of Dunbar's poems, "make de soun' come right," if he's got the "tu'uns an' twistin's / Fu to make it sweet an' light" ("When Malin-dy Sings," p. 82), the Tuskegeean could move his head in affirmation. Unlike Bradshaw, however, Washington does not disappoint his audience with British accents, or with pale lamentations of bitter clay and lengthy miles. Instead, he struts minstrel stuff so grandly that there is no choice but to lay twenty thousand on him—"I will be very glad to pay the bills for the library building," etc. The sage of Tuskegee understood that there were mnemonic *sounds*, nonsense syllables, so defining of "the Negro" in American life that they were inescapable if one was earnestly to address "the Negro question." And in the Afro-American literary domain, the spokesperson who shared Mr. Washington's understanding was Charles Waddell Chesnutt.

The first edition of *The Conjure Woman*, Chesnutt's 1899 collection of short stories, immediately reveals what might be called the graphics of minstrelsy. On the cover, a venerably comic black man who is bald and possessed of big ears, rough features, and a great deal of woolly white hair merges—not unintentionally—with two rather malevolent looking caricatures of rabbits. The Houghton, Mifflin and Company designers outdid themselves in suggesting the link between Chesnutt's content and that of the ever popular Joel Chandler Harris's "Uncle Remus" and the crafty Brer Rabbit of Afro-American folk ancestry. There is, to be sure, justification for regarding Chesnutt's work as an expressive instance of the traditional trickster rabbit tales of black folklore, since his main character Uncle Julius manages to acquire gains by strategies that are familiar to students of Brer Rabbit. The real force of *The Conjure Woman*, however, does not reside in a febrile replay of an old Harris tune. Rather, the collection's strength lies in the deep and intensive recoding of form that marks its stories. The work is best characterized as a drama of transformation.

In a letter from Chesnutt to Walter Hines Page in 1898 we find the following:

Speaking of dialect, it is almost a despairing task to write it. . . . The fact is, of course, that there is no such thing as a Negro dialect; that what we call by that name is the attempt to express, with such a degree of phonetic correctness as to suggest *the sound,* English pronounced as an ignorant old southern Negro would be supposed to speak it. [Pp. 94–95, my emphasis]

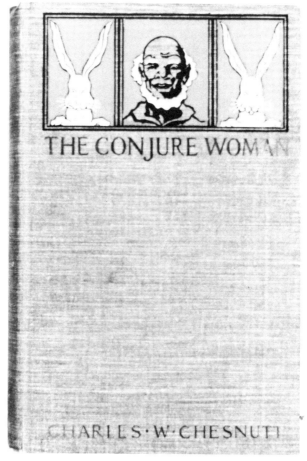

Cover design of Charles Chesnutt's short story collection *The Conjure Woman.*

In these reflections shared with one of the most influential literary editors and brokers of his era, Chesnutt shrewdly gives and takes in a single, long breath. He unequivocally states that the task of the spokesperson who would render black life adequately is to "suggest the *sound*." At the same time, he knows to whom he is speaking and promptly gives Page something for his fancy—"an ignorant old southern Negro." In a phrase, then, we have encoded the injunction from Chesnutt to *heed the sound* and a disclaimer to Page that says there is no need—really, boss—to fear the sound: it is still that of an ignorant old darky.

Nothing, of course, could be farther from the truth. Chesnutt had been aware for years that the plantation tradition in American letters and even more studied efforts by white authors to write about the Afro-American were inadequate and frequently idiotic. He had also been fully aware that what editors like Page passed off as "Negrolife in story" was radically opposed to the story he wanted to tell. Listen again as Chesnutt gives and takes in a single breath.

Having been dithyrambic about the March 1899 issue of *Atlantic* in a letter to Page, he then says, "The dialect story is one of the sort of Southern stories that make me feel it is *my duty* to write a different sort, and yet I did not lay it down without a tear of genuine emotion" (p. 107, my emphasis). As an Afro-American spokesperson, Chesnutt was acutely aware of "his duty" to preserve fidelity to the *sound* of African ancestors and the phonics of their descendants in the "country districts." Rather than producing a simpleminded set of trickster stories framed by the ponderous pretensions of a white Ohio Buckeye as narrator, therefore, he offered a world of sounds and sweet airs that resonates with the transformative power of *conjure*.

Conjure is the transatlantic religion of diasporic and Afro-American masses in the New World. Descended from *vodun*, an African religion in which the priestess holds supreme power, conjure's name in Haiti and the Caribbean is *voodoo*. The force that transmutes and transforms in Chesnutt's volume of stories is the *root work* and empowering mediations of *The Spirit* that mark the efforts of voodoo's Houngans or conjure's "two-headed doctors." In the stories of *The Conjure Woman*, we find a struggle in progress as the white, Ohio narrator who has moved to southern "country districts" strives to provide empirical explanations—a certain species of philosophical "nonsense"—as a reassuring mask for the myriad manifestations of Uncle Julius's "spirit work." The seemingly comic old "uncle," in turn, ceaselessly transmits sounds about a cruel order of bondage that has transformed African harmony, as idealized and serene as a Dan mask, into family separation, floggings, and commercial negotiations. But even as Julius relays his sound, he introduces, valorizes, and validates a *root* phonics that is vastly different from the sounds of the Ohio narrator. The *difference* is conjure. For conjure is a power of transformation that causes definitions of "form" as fixed and comprehensible "thing" to dissolve. Black men, considered by slavery as "things" or "chattel personal," are transformed through conjure into seasonal vegetation figures, or trees, or gray wolves. White men, in turn, are transmuted into surly and abused "noo niggers." A black child is changed into a hummingbird and a mockingbird. A black woman becomes a cat, and an elderly black man's clubfoot is a reminder of his transformation—under a conjurer's "revenge"—into a mule.

The fluidity of *The Conjure Woman's* world, symbolized by such metamorphoses, is a function of the black narrator's mastery of form. The old man knows the sounds that are dear to the hearts of his white boss and his wife, and he presents them with conjuring efficaciousness. In effect, he presents a world in which "dialect" masks the drama of African spirituality challenging and changing the disastrous transformations of slavery. A continuation of this historic masking ritual is at work in the "present" universe of *The Conjure Woman* (the space/time in which Julius relates his stories to Ohioans). For throughout all of the volume's stories the *sound* of African ancestry operates at a low, signifying, and effective register *behind* the mask of a narrational dialect that, in Chesnutt's words, is "no . . . thing." Finally, what is sharply modified by the transformative soundings of the work are the dynamics of lordship and bondage as a whole. When the work concludes, Julius has obtained a job, use of a building on the Ohioan's property for black community organizational purposes, employment for his grandson, and (possibly) profits from a duplicitous horse trade. In a sense, one might say that Julius has secured—in the very heart of the country districts—an enclave in which a venerable Afro-American spirit can sound off. During all of the black narrator's tellings, the white Ohioan believes the stories are merely expressive of a minstrel type. He views Julius as, at best, a useful entertainment, one who can do odd jobs *and* tell stories. He considers him, at worst, an agent of annoyance and craftiness—never as a potent force of African transformations that can not be comprehended or controlled by Western philosophy.

But what is meant here by Western philosophy? The Ohioan's reading at the beginning of "The Gray Wolf's Ha'nt" provides an indication of the kind of rational control the white man seeks in the face of formal transmutations. He reads the following passage to his wife "with pleasure":

> "The difficulty of dealing with transformations so many-sided as those which all existences have undergone, or are undergoing, is such as to make a complete and deductive interpretation almost hopeless. So to grasp the total process of redistribution of matter and motion as to see simultaneously its several necessary results in their actual independence is scarcely possible. There is, however, a mode of rendering the process as a whole tolerably comprehensible."[35]

"John," says his wife, "I wish you would stop reading that *nonsense* and see who that is coming up the lane" (p.

164, my emphasis). Indeed, the process of "redistribution" suggested in the passage is philosophically incomprehensible in Western terms, especially if that very redistribution is being effected from behind the minstrel mask—with the sound of minstrelsy seeming to dominate—by an African sensibility. The transformations wrought in and by Julius's tales are *conjure changes* necessitated by a bizarre economics of slavery. Only spiritual transformations of the "slave" self as well as the "master" self ("Mars Jeems's Nightmare") in a universe governed by *root work* (a work that demands that adherents pay in full to the priestess Aunt Peggy) will enable the progress and survival of a genuinely Afro-American *sound*.

Julius's voice is in fact a function of conjure and a conjuring function. It allows Chesnutt—who, like Julius, is a North Carolinian who has heard "de tale fer twenty-five years . . . and ain't got no 'casion for ter 'spute it"—to *sound* a common tale of Afro-American transformative resourcefulness under the guise of an ole "uncle" speaking *nonsense*. The power of Julius and Chesnutt resides in the change they work on their audiences. They put, so to speak, their white hearers through changes. Listen to the Ohioan's wife at the conclusion of "The Conjurer's Revenge"—the tale that appears in advance of the one in which her husband attempts to read "transformation." At the story's close, she condemns Julius's narration as follows: "That story does not appeal to me, Uncle Julius, and is not up to your usual mark. . . . In fact, it seems to me like nonsense" (p. 127). When the next story opens—"Sis' Becky's Pickaninny"— the mistress has fallen morosely ill and neither "novels" read by John, nor "plantation songs" sung by "the hands" can effect a cure.

In comes Uncle Julius with his *conjure,* and when his tale of Sis' Becky is done—a tale whose moral the wife is able to supply, bringing her and the teller into expressive accord— she begins to improve. *Conjure* is also known, of course, as folk medicine. "My wife's condition," says the Ohioan, "took a turn for the better from this very day, and she was soon on the way to ultimate recovery" (p. 160). Can it come as a surprise that the wife's characterization of two opposed *phonics*—Western philosophical rationalism meant to comprehend and control fluidity, and African conjure meant to move the spirit through a fluid repertoire of "forms"—grants the nod to *conjure?* The designation *nonsense* falls with a heavy thump upon rationalism's polysyllables at the commencement of "The Gray Wolf's Ha'nt." And we know by this token that Julius (like his creator) has played a mojo hand with the deft brilliance of a master of form.

What moves through Chesnutt's collection is the sound of a southern black culture that knew it had to *re-form* a slave world created by the West's willful transformation of Africans into chattel. Conjure's spirit work moves behind—within, and through—the mask of minstrelsy to ensure survival, to operate changes, to acquire necessary resources for continuance, and to cure a sick world. At the first appearance of Chesnutt's "conjure" stories in the *Atlantic,* (and in his correspondence, the word "conjure" is always in quotes, protected as a *tricky* or transformative sign—masked), a white audience thought they were hearing merely entertaining syllables of a lovable darky. The turn-of-the-century writer's goal, however, was "a different story" for a different world, and he achieved this black southern eloquence in a discourse unequaled in his day.

6

Chesnutt's effectiveness as a "modern" lay in his ability to give the trick to white expectations, securing publication for creative work that carries a deep-rooted African sound. Dunbar's strength where authentic Afro-American expressivity was concerned lay in an entirely different direction. Rather than aspiring to a mastery of form like Washington and Chesnutt, the black poet chose the *deformation of mastery* as his strategy. And in this choice, he followed the august example of that genius from Great Barrington, Dr. W. E. B. DuBois. If we turn for a moment to observations on biological "form," we can distinguish graphically between what I call the mastery of form and the strategies of DuBois and Dunbar.

The zoologist H. B. Cott writes:

> A . . . factor influencing form . . . is an animal's appearance, considered in relation to the visual perception of other animals, whether of the same or different species. In the struggle for existence, two primary necessities for life are security and sustenance. If an animal is to survive, it must in one way or another obtain food and at the same time avoid being eaten. . . . The devices by means of which animals achieve these three ends are almost infinitely various. Many, themselves bewildering in their varied modes of action and application to the day-to-day needs of survival, fall into a class by themselves—in that they exert their influence upon other animals from a distance, by sound, by sight, or by scent. To such characters the term "allaesthetic" has been applied.[36]

Though this passage sounds suspiciously like nature "red in tooth and claw," I believe one can be reassured by the example of the praying mantis as an insect whose "allaesthetic" characteristics allow it to master the form of the green stalk so completely that predators—at a distance, and even close at hand—cannot distinguish its edibility. Cott elaborates:

> The nature of allaesthetic characters, and the "public" in relation to which they have evolved, vary widely: on the visual side, the phenomena fall broadly into three main categories—namely, concealment, disguise, and advertisement; on the functional side, these elusive, deceptive or attractive features are variously concerned with other organisms of the habitat—whether predators or prey, mates or rivals, parents or offspring.[37]

Allaesthetic characteristics, in short, are biological *masks*—elusive constellations designed to enhance inclusive fitness. Adopting a shorthand, we might say in fact that the difference between the mastery of form and the deformation of mastery is that between a praying mantis, or rabbit (did you ever attempt to follow the movements of an autumn hare through sedge-brown, October woods?), and a gorilla.

The mastery of form conceals, disguises, floats like a trickster butterfly in order to sting like a bee. The deformation of mastery, by contrast, is Morris Day singing "Jungle Love," advertising, with certainty, his unabashed *badness*—which is not always conjoined with violence. *Deformation* is a go(uer)rilla action in the face of acknowledged adversaries. It produces sounds radically different from those of, say, Sade, whose almost mumbled initial exposition gives way to subdued (but scandalously signifying) lyrics in "Smooth Operator."

The deformation of mastery is fully at work in gorilla "display." Man—the master of "civilization"—enters forests and triggers a response. The display is described by Colin Groves:

> The full display is extremely impressive and quite terrify-
> ing except to another gorilla. . . . [The gorilla] stands or
> sits on the ground, and begins to hoot. Suddenly he
> stops; unexpectedly he turns his head, plucks a leaf with
> his lips and holds it between them . . . the hoots get fast-
> er and faster, the gorilla rises on his hindlegs. . . . Still
> standing erect, he runs sideways a few yards, bringing
> himself up short and slapping and tearing at the vegeta-
> tion with great sideways sweeps of the arms. At last, as if
> to bring the display to a final close, he thumps the
> ground with the open palm of one or both hands, and
> drops back onto all fours.[38]

Such displays present the type of allaesthetic mask that Cott calls *phaneric*. Rather than concealing or disguising in the manner of the *cryptic* mask (a colorful mastery of codes), the phaneric mask is meant to advertise. It distinguishes rather than conceals. It secures territorial advantage and heightens a group's survival possibilities.

The gorilla's deformation is made possible by his superior knowledge of the landscape and the loud assertion of pos-session that he makes. It is, of course, the latter—the "hoots" of assurance that remain incomprehensible to in-truders—that produce a notion (in the intruder's mind and vocabulary) of "deformity." An "alien" *sound* gives birth to notions of the indigenous—say, Africans, or Afro-Ameri-cans—as *deformed*.

Two things, then, can be stated about the dynamics of deformation: first, the indigenous comprehend the territory within their own vale/veil more fully than any intruder. ("The kingdom is divided into many provinces or districts, in one of the most remote and fertile of which, I was born, in the year 1745, situated in a charming fruitful *vale*, named Essaka." Thus writes Olaudah Equiano the African. And W. E. B. DuBois provides echoes in his own prefatory words to a gorilla literacy: "And, finally, need I add that I who speak here am bone of the bone and flesh of the flesh of them that live within the Veil?").[39] The vale/Veil, one might assert, is for the indigenous *language* itself.

Second, the indigenous *sound* appears monstrous and deformed *only* to the intruder. In the popular domain, the intruder's response is King Kong (or Mr. T); in literature, the trope most frequently visited by "alien" writers and their adversaries is the hooting deformed of Shakespeare's *Tempest*.

Caliban, like a maroon in Jamaican hills or Nat Turner preparing his phaneric exit from the Great Dismal Swamp of the American South, focuses a drama of deformation that authors such as George Lamming, James Baldwin, and, of course, William Melvin Kelley have found suggestive for their own situations. What then of deformity/deformation and Caliban?

7

If one claims, following a post-structuralist line, that to possess the "gift" of language is to be possessed, then one immediately situates him or herself in a domain familiar to the diaspora. *Possession* operates both in the spirit work of voodoo and in the dread slave and voodoo economics perpetuated by the West. What is involved in possession, in either case, is supplementarity—the immediately mediating appearance, as spectre or shadow, of a second and secondary "self." In specifically diasporic terms, "being possessed" (as slave, but also as a BEING POSSESSED) is more than a necessary doubling or inscribed "otherness" of the *con-scripted* (those who come, as necessity, *with* writing). For in the diaspora, the possessed are governed not simply by *script* but also by productive conditions that render their entire play a *tripling*.

Caliban speaks his possession as a metacurse:

> You taught me language; and my profit on't
> Is, I know how to curse. The red plague rid you
> For learning me your language.[40]

Caliban's utterance is "meta" because its semantics are marked by economies (implied or explicit) of *ob-scenity*— they speak *against* the scene of an intruder's tongue. Not "self" discovery, but the impossibility of feeling anything other than cursed by language is the sense of Caliban's utterance. For his self-assurance is not at issue. He has always known the forms (the morphology) of his indigenous vale, reminding the intruding Prospero of his role in showing "thee all the qualities o' th' isle, / The fresh springs, brine-pits, barren place and fertile" (1.2.339–41). Further, he scarcely lacks self-certainty regarding transformations wrought by the Western magician's intrusion. He and Prospero are alike "kings" victimized by *usurpation,* which is, in effect, the force and theme that moves the action of the play. The preeminent reason that Caliban is the metatactician of *The Tempest,* however, is his morphophonemics—his situation vis-à-vis sound variations ("sounds and sweet airs")—which are truly foundational.

In his essay *Nature,* Ralph Waldo Emerson writes: "Nature is the vehicle of thought."[41] On Caliban's island, there could be no signifying whatsoever were it not for the indigenous inhabitant's instruction in the language (veil/vale) of nature. Seeking a new master, Caliban ebulliently promises the island's semantics to the scurrilous Stephano: "I'll show you the best springs"; "I prithee, let me bring thee where crabs grow. . . . Show thee a jay's nest, and instruct thee how / To snare the nimble marmoset" (2.2.160, 167–70). Sycorax's son is the adept instructor in natural "forms."

"Every appearance in nature," continues Emerson, "corresponds to some state of the mind, and that state of the mind can only be described by presenting that natural appearance as its picture."[42] The icons or pictures of Caliban's island reflect the usurpations of the Renaissance West—a social world of displaced knowledge-seekers that mocked (to distraction) honestly salvific people like Gonzalo. A shared nature *as* language—as a fruitful ecology of communication—was, thus, subjected to usurpation by men who refused to brook difference. Tyranny demanded self-sameness, subjugation, appropriated labor—even from the seemingly suitable suitor. (Ferdinand becomes the "other" in the woodpile to qualify as Miranda's groom.) The "tempest," then, is, veritably, a havoc wreaked by mastery; it disrupts "natural" order—blunts "sounds and sweet airs, that give delight, and hurt not" (3.2.134). The Western Renaissance "storm" displaces in fact the witch as worker of sounding magic and releases, in her place, the comprador spirit Ariel who aids Propero's male manipulations.

The tripling of Caliban vis-à-vis writing as supplementarity is implicit in Gonzalo's vision of *difference:* "I would by contraries / Execute all things"; "All things in common Nature should produce . . . treason, felony, / Sword, pike, knife, gun, or need of any engine, / Would I not have" (2.1.143–44, 155–58). In brief, the "fool" would have the isle widely pre-Prosperian, revising or deforming the contraries of Western civilization in order to return to a "natural" signification. Such a world would witness Caliban not as student of "culture as a foreign language" (CFL, as it were), but rather as an instructor in a first voice, resonant with "a thousand twangling instruments" *in* nature. Caliban's position as metacurser derives from his knowledge that his cursedness is a function of his own largesse as signifier, as a man in tune with *first* meanings. "Curs'd be I that did so!" is his judgment on his willingness to barter his signs for the white magician's language.

The West Indian novelist George Lamming argues that Prospero gives Caliban language and thus controls his conceptual field through a dubious gift.[43] And James Baldwin seems to accept Lamming's point of view when he writes:

> The Negro problem [meaning, surely, the actual *sound* of a sui generis life in America] is nearly inaccessible. It is not only written about so widely; it is written about so badly. It is quite possible to say that the price the Negro pays for becoming articulate is to find himself, at length, with nothing to be articulate about. ("You taught me language," says Caliban to Prospero, "and my profit on't is I know how to curse.")[44]

Baldwin, like Lamming, asserts that the field of vision surrounding those considered "deformed" is overdetermined by the assumption that *sounds* of protective display are crude protests, or laments.

There is a sense, however, in which we are compelled to see what Baldwin, Lamming, and others consider a dilemma as the motivating challenge of *writing* as a project in and for itself. For the original island dweller—son of Sycorax—is aware of a cursed "self" cursing a notion of "self" that assumes that sounds of the phaneric mask are, like the conditions of language itself, alienating and fearful. This awareness, of course, calls into question the intruder's very definitions of "self" (worth). What batters our ears—if Caliban is newly interpreted—is the three-personed god of "natural" meanings, morphophonemics, and, most importantly, metamorphoses. The Afro-American spokesperson who would perform a deformation of mastery shares the task of Sycorax's son insofar as he or she must transform an obscene situation, a cursed and tripled metastatus, into a signal self/cultural expression. The birth of such a self is never simply a coming into being, but always, also, a release from a BEING POSSESSED. The practice of a phaneric, diasporic expressivity is both a metadiscourse on linguistic investiture and a lesson in the metaphorical "worm holing," as it were—the tunneling out of the black holes of possession and "tight places" of old clothes, into, perhaps, a new universe. Black writers, one might say, are always on *display*, writing a black renaissance and righting a Western Renaissance that was, in the words of Ralph Ellison's preacher in *Invisible Man*, "most black, brother, most black." Language, insists Jacques Derrida, is a "possibility founded on the general possibility of writing."[45]

The deformation of mastery refuses a master's *nonsense*. It returns—often transmuting "standard" syllables—to the common sense of the tribe. Its relationship to masks is radically different from that of the mastery of form. The spirit house occupying the deformer is not minstrelsy, but the sound and space of an African ancestral past. For the Afro-American spokesperson, the most engaging repository for deformation's sounding work is the fluid and multiform mask of African ancestry. At the dawn of the twentieth century, the most articulate adherent of African sound was W. E. B. DuBois.

The Souls of Black Folk announces in its very title that an "other world" nonsense will not be countenanced. A nation, a FOLK manifold in spirit (note the plurality of "soul" captured by its *s*), will be the subject of the black spokesperson's narrative.[46] Afro-American songs appropriately called "spirituals" provide sound for a ritual that begins with the title. The whole of *Souls* moves in fact toward the moment in chapter fourteen when the text becomes a sounding score—when a phaneric narrator reveals that he *knows the score* where lordship and deformity are concerned.

The governing metaphor of *Souls* is the "Veil." The Veil signifies a barrier of American racial segregation that keeps Afro-Americans always behind a color line—disoriented— prey to divided aims, dire economic circumstances, haphazard educational opportunities, and frustrated intellectual ambitions. In the penultimate vision of *Souls* that occurs in chapter fourteen, this Veil is rent. In an act of wish fulfillment par excellence, the narrator envisions an "Eternal Good" acting to compel American justice. A merger of youth and age, African-American cultural anima and Western high culture, Negro masses and Negro thinking classes is the sounding result of this rending of the Veil. Such fruitful and empowering mergers of long-standing dualities carry the following sound:

> If somewhere in this whirl and chaos of things there dwells Eternal Good, pitiful yet masterful, then anon in His good time America shall rend the Veil and the prisoned shall go free. Free, free as the sunshine trickling down the morning into these high windows of mine, free as yonder fresh young voices welling up to me from the caverns of brick and mortar below—swelling with song, instinct with life, tremulous treble and darkening bass. My children, my little children, are singing to the sunshine, and thus they sing:[47]

At this moment in my text, I am compelled to leave an incompletion.

The space is metonymic for the larger space that DuBois leaves in his own text. His space is filled by the score of "Let Us Cheer the Weary Traveller." The song constitutes ancient African-American *sound* performed by a new generation of black folk. It signals a conflation of African and American selves on the ritual ground of a black southern university—a locus, or space, that DuBois pictures as the only oasis for a FOLK whose masses occupy the "country districts" of the South. The merger of old disjunctions and the forecast of a future unity of aims that will bring new harmony to America are comprehensible only when we regard *The Souls of Black Folk* as a profoundly southern book.

Outside its intensely regional cast, *Souls* is virtually unclassifiable. The work is certainly not an autobiography, nor is it merely a collection of random or fugitive essays. In a sense, it could be labeled a spiritual meditation—a numinous passage through spiritual landscapes. But the word "meditation" suggests a passivity that is nowhere apparent in the work. I think the phrase "cultural performance" is perhaps the most apt classification.

Assuming the space of a long-standing cultural sound, DuBois polyphonically (employing syllables from Prospero's art, science, economics, sociology, and politics, as well as myriad Afro-American accents) dances before our eyes the drama of RACE in the modern world. His performance is dioramic; it offers a bright, sounding spiritual display of men, women, institutions, doctrines, debates, follies, tragedies, hopes, expectations, and policies that combine to form a "problem."

The DuBoisian voice ceaselessly invokes ancestral spirits and ancient formulas that move toward an act of cultural triumph. In fact, I define the Afro-American spiritual as synonymous with the African mask here because DuBois's nar-

Score of "Let Us Cheer the Weary Traveller" as it appears in
The Souls of Black Folk.

rator seems so patently self-conscious in his repeated use of "Sorrow Songs" or spirituals as masterful respositories of an African cultural spirit. We are instructed as follows:

> The songs are indeed the siftings of centuries; the music is far more ancient than the words, and in it we can trace here and there signs of development. My grandfather's grandmother was seized by an evil Dutch trader two centuries ago; and coming to the valleys of the Hudson and Housatonic, black, little, and lithe, she shivered and shrank in the harsh north winds, looked longingly at the hills, and often crooned a heathen melody to the child between her knees, thus: [P. 380]

Again, I am compelled to leave a metonymic gap, a space filled by sound alone. For DuBois introduces, after his "thus," the score and words—*Do ba-na co-ba, ge-ne me, ge-ne me!*—of an ancient African spiritual repository. Expository words thus fissure into resonant sound.

Music, in its venerability, is held to be "far more ancient than the words." Hence, the spirituals stand as counter and deforming forms in relation not only to minstrel nonsense (they predate and give the *sounding* lie to such idiocy) but also to Western verbal arrangements. Each chapter of *Souls* is prefaced by a fragment of the score—the actual *sounding* music—of a spiritual as well as by a *written* passage from the work of a Western poet. The Western letter—Prospero's *parole*—always appears first. One can veritably hear this written letter erased by the spiritual *langue* of Caliban's singing. The singing is neither an exotic nor a passive absorption of an intruder's dubious linguistic arrangements. Rather, it is a type of phaneric cultural display coequal with the narrative voice that sounds toward the conclusion of *Souls:*

> Your country? How came it yours? Before the Pilgrims landed we were here. Here we have brought our three gifts and mingled them with yours: a gift of story and song—soft, stirring melody in an ill-harmonized and unmelodious land; the gift of sweat and brawn to beat back the wilderness, conquer the soil, and lay the founda-

tions of this vast economic empire two hundred years earlier than your weak hands could have done it; the third, a gift of the Spirit. Around us the history of the land has centered for thrice a hundred years. [Pp. 386–87]

Not only do we catch the incantational sounds of gorilla display, but we also hear (returning not harsh nor grating) syllables of the putatively "deformed"—sounds of those who in Aimé Césaire's phrase are held to "have invented nothing."[48] These sounds bespeak nativity: "This land," the narrator soundingly proclaims, "is mine by right of my having been always already here."

Thus the sounding figurations of Caliban are discovered as script(ural) revenue of New World writing. James Baldwin once asserted during a dramatic cultural performance of his own, "He who would enter the twenty-first century, must come by way of me."[49] Similarly, DuBois's *Souls* implies that any conceivable global modernism in an age where "the color line" is preeminent must be articulated through Caliban's expressive traditions—traditions that sing a joyful song on the far side of an acknowledgment of the fictional character of "self" and "other."

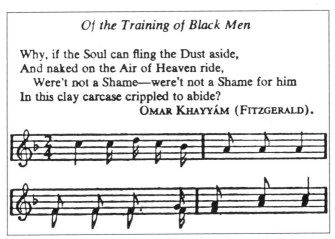

Title, epigraph, and partial score of an Afro-American spiritual, from *The Souls of Black Folk*.

I earlier suggested that one of the fittest classifications for *Souls* is regional. I believe that it is DuBois's struggle to re-figure the South as it appears in *Up from Slavery* that necessitates his appropriation of an African sound and his stance as a deformer of Western expressive arrangements. Washington's South is a place of reconciliation. Sectional bitterness has disappeared; whites and blacks, under proper terms, work together. Agriculture and industry are compatible. Capital and labor (if unions are eradicated) may unite in the fruitful production of a New South. Within this larger iconography, the Tuskegee orator envisions a black Eden—a "skills center" for Afro-Americans of the "country districts." In order to foster the reconciliation that he sees so mightily and effectively at work, Washington is willing to build and oversee his *Negro Paradise* at Tuskegee and to reconcile whatever he thinks of as an "authentic" self with demands of a larger world from which he must secure venture capital. In some ways, his narrative constitutes a lying exorcism of patent realities, a fictive purgation of evil in order to allow the work of Tuskegee to take form. Hence, he expunges the Ku Klux Klan: "To-day there are no such organizations in the South, and the fact that such ever existed is almost forgotten by both races. There are few places in the South now where public sentiment would permit such organizations to exist" (p. 71).

Now it is not the case that *Souls* is free of the kind of conciliatory "hands across the color line" rhetoric that marks *Up from Slavery*. We listen as DuBois reflects on relationships between sons of masters and of men:

> I should be the last to withhold sympathy from the white South in its efforts to solve its intricate social problems. I freely acknowledge that it is possible, and sometimes best, that a partially undeveloped people should be ruled by the best of their stronger and better neighbors for their own good, until such time as they can start and fight the world's battles alone. I have already pointed out how sorely in need of such economic and spiritual guid-

ance the emancipated Negro was, and I am quite willing to admit that if the representatives of the best white Southern public opinion were the ruling and guiding powers in the South to-day the conditions indicated would be fairly well fulfilled. [P. 329]

There are definite shades in this DuBoisian utterance of the mastery of form. One looks from a scandalous Washington to a lying DuBois and cannot tell the difference. But if there are multiple instances in *Souls* of DuBois's awareness that whites had to be mollified, there are far more instances of the author's sounding awareness that the very existence of a productive South is contingent upon an intelligent critique of Washingtonian geographies—geographies that are scarcely reconcilable with DuBoisian territories of Afro-American spiritual imaginings. And that is the very word one wants for DuBois's effort—*critique*. Defined as a philosophical term, the critique is a considered detailing of arguments and an amassing and interpretation of evidence designed to refigure prevailing notions of a topic or area of inquiry. The word and process take force from Kant's usage and suggest the dialectic between Hegel and Marx as an inversion—or standing on its feet—of an extant view.

DuBois's inversions of an extant Southern problematic begin with his title, which suggests spirit and duration rather than a historically and materially grounded "slavery" as the Afro-American's point of commencement. Further, *Souls* does not present an unwashed black mob in country districts devoid of toothbrushes, given to razor play, and, yes, nonsense syllables of minstrelsy. Instead, *Souls* presents a FOLK.

The narrator's cultural performance, therefore, can give life to a sign ("folk") that connotes a pretechnological but nonetheless vital stage of human development toward ideals of CULTURE. A FOLK is always, out of the very necessities of definition, possessed of a guiding or tutelary spirit—an immanent quality of aspiration that is fittingly sounded in its treasured rituals, in its spirit houses or masks of performance. And for DuBois, the immanence of black folk resides in what he defines in "Of the Meaning of Progress" as a "shadow of an unconscious moral heroism that would willingly give all of life to make life broader, deeper, and fuller" (p. 254).

"Immanent," indeed, one might say, since the trait embodied by Josie, the heroine of the essay, is a "shadow" of something that is itself "unconscious." Yet DuBois transforms this immanence into tangible form. It shows most concretely as "the longing to know, to be a student in the great school [Fisk University] at Nashville" (p. 255). In short, "moral heroism" translates, in DuBoisian cultural performance, as a desire for university education. Such a desire (and its object) lead to the inculcation of CULTURE. Culture, in turn, is an advanced stage in a march to civilization. It instills the broad view and a spirit of self-sacrifice leading to brotherhood.

In an essay written some years ago, I defined DuBois as a "Man of Culture" and evaluated the signal importance of *Souls* as its depiction of a black man of culture.[50] Certainly, the accolades DuBois's work has received from successive generations of Afro-American "men of culture" seems to reinforce that claim. But as I ponder today the effects of *Souls*, I am certain that CULTURE is less important as a sign defining the work than the phrase CULTURAL PERFORMANCE—a phrase, as I have implied, that always signifies a distinctively Afro-American sounding of events.

"Culture" in DuBois's text is drawn in recognizable Western terms:

> In the morning [at Atlanta University], when the sun is golden, the clang of the day-bell brings the hurry and laughter of three hundred young hearts from hall and street, and from the busy city below,—children all dark and heavy-haired,—to join their clear young voices in the music of the morning sacrifice. In a half-dozen classrooms they gather then,—here to follow the love-song of Dido, here to listen to the tale of Troy divine; there to

wander among the stars, there to wander among men and nations,—and elsewhere other well-worn ways of knowing this queer world. Nothing new, no time-saving devices,—simply old time-glorified methods of delving for Truth, and searching out the hidden beauties of life, and learning the good of living. The riddle of existence is the college curriculum that was laid before the Pharaohs, that was taught in the groves by Plato, that formed the *trivium* and *quadrivium,* and is today laid before the freedman's sons by Atlanta University. [Pp. 266–67]

Not only is "culture" a "curriculum" of the best that has been thought and known, but it is also an attitude of free inquiry, a free play of the mind about all ideas.

In the final analysis, however, DuBois realizes that such culture as the West projects must be energized by a sounding *on, within, and beyond* "culture" by "clear young voices in the music of the morning." Young, aspiring, melodious "moral heroism" from black "country districts" comprises the most achieved and potentially productive realization of a folk spirit in active operation. The university—the black, southern university—is not characterized by halls of ivy but rather by "chapel[s] of melody" (p. 258).

The words "chapel of melody" appear in "Of the Meaning of Progress" as a sign for Fisk University. In his concluding essay, DuBois writes:

> To me Jubilee Hall seemed ever made of the songs [spirituals] themselves, and its bricks were red with the blood and dust of toil. Out of them rose for me morning, noon, and night, bursts of wonderful melody, full of the voices of my brothers and sisters, full of the voices of the past. [P. 378]

The extraordinary merging in this passage of university, song, blood and dust of toil, and bonded voices of black folk brothers and sisters signals the real topography of DuBois's landscape. In the *vale* of the country districts, there may be tears and trouble. ("We've had a heap of trouble since you've been away," Josie's mother tells the young school-teacher when he revisits the vale ten years after his first entry.) There may be defeated dreams, racist suppression, and lamentable death. But there is also a longing to build edifices of culture out of melodies of ancient spiritual song. If there is elegy—a constant death's-head—resident on the southern landscapes presented in *Souls* (think, as the critic Kimberly Benston suggested to me,[51] of Josie's demise, the deaths of the white and black Johns, the passing of DuBois's first born), then there is also the rife potential of *re-membering* song.

The folk not only come to the domain of culture but also refigure the very notion of "culture" for the modern world. Their immanent moral heroism and spirituality are best sounded among traditional Western masterpieces as a way of transforming such artifacts (and themselves) into resources for a world where mastery has been deformed. The Fisk Jubilee Singers, who carried the actual sound of Afro-American spiritual strivings—the articulate cries of slaves to the world—before enraptured audiences both at home and abroad, offer a trope for the merger of immanent folk heroism, Western cultural masterpieces, and the sound of African spirituality that rends the Veil and portends salvific edifices of melody for the South. The narrator reflects:

> So in 1871 the pilgrimage of the Fisk Jubilee Singers began. North to Cincinnati they rode,—four half-clothed black boys and five girl-women,—led by a man with a cause and a purpose. . . . They went, fighting cold and starvation, shut out of hotels, and cheerfully sneered at, ever northward; and ever the magic of their song kept thrilling hearts, until a burst of applause in the Congregational Council at Oberlin revealed them to the world. [P. 379]

These "half-clothed" singers are *the folk* come to college, engaged in cultural production and exchange. "Seven years they sang, and brought back a hundred and fifty thousand

The original Fisk Jubilee Singers. (Courtesy of Fisk University Library, Special Collections.)

dollars to found Fisk University" (p. 379). The black southern university is, thus, rightly termed a "chapel of melody," a reverent spot on the southern landscape representing an Afro-American expressivity which lends to definitions of culture a new resonance.

DuBois's South sings. Washington's South exposits. DuBois's South, through the agency of Afro-American *cultural performance,* is conjoined to centuries of moral heroism, dedicated sacrifice, and earnest inquiry into the riddle of life. A black-bestowed definition, or *sounding,* offers the *only* promise of spirituality in a world increasingly moved by work and money. Yet, dollars too are, ironically, a function of Afro-American spirituality. The Jubilee Singers return with 150,000 dollars, a veritable fortune in their era.

The most salient distinction between DuBois's deformation and Washington's mastery is, finally, that between a landscape that *sounds* an ancient, authentic song and a half-fictionalized expository geography that compels the sounding of half-fictionalized nonsense. Both *Souls* and *Up from Slavery*, however, provide strategies that re-sound in the Afro-American 1920s as a generation of black spokespersons work within the field of expressive possibilities (a world set essentially on southern terrain) created by the fluid and always interdependent relationship between mastery and deformation. Washington remains the spokesperson *on behalf* of the folk (who, really, are not a FOLK in his account); DuBois, by melodious contrast, lifts his voice and transmutes his text into the FOLK's singing. If Washington provides a speaking manual, then DuBois offers a singing book.

Before turning to the work of the Harlem 1920s, it is well to round off remarks on Paul Laurence Dunbar by saying simply that his novel *The Sport of the Gods*, which is likewise an expressive coding of southern environs, finds its voice in the calm face of an ironical, or satirical, African mask deriding all minstrel forms. The speaking voice of Dunbar's narrative is aware from the outset that a new "fiction" is wanted if the south is to become a world prefiguring a modern liberation of the spirit. "Fiction," says the novel's narrator, "has said so much in regret of the old days when there were plantations and overseers and masters and slaves, that it was good to come upon such a household as Berry Hamilton's, if for no other reason than that it afforded a relief from the monotony of tiresome iteration."[52]

I have detailed the entailments of this opening statement in a recent essay[53] and can only briefly add here that what marks the narrator as a practitioner of deformation—a phaneric sounder—is the irony that deconstructs such forms and institutions as the plantation tradition, southern artistic representation, white southern myths of a Cavalier gentility, the inanities of black theatricals, and American journalism's putative dedication to evidentiary fairness. A "mad" wailing– akin to that which concludes Faulkner's *Absalom, Absalom!*—is the result of the narrator's deformative labors. The new form that produces this cry is a *sounding* on folly and excess; the sound is filtered through a persona or mask that looks like Eshu the very god of Irony. And the overall sound, strategy, and effect of Dunbar's labors brings his 1901 novel into fine accord with the bad "bookooing" of the inimitable Ishmael Reed.[54] Caliban is in control, metamorphosing a linguistics of mastery with masterful sound.

8

A nation's emergence is always predicated on the construction of a field of meaningful sounds. Just as infants babble through a welter of phones to achieve the phonemics of a native language, so conglomerates of human beings seeking national identity engage myriad sounds in order to achieve a vocabulary of *national* possibilities. The codes, statutes, declarations, articles, amendments, and constitution of colonial America constitute, for example, what Sacvan Bercovitch calls a "logocracy." In Bercovitch's reading, the American nation as such is but an edifice and enterprise of distinctive and distinguishing words.

Similarly, efforts of turn-of-the-century black spokespersons provide tactics, strategies, and sounds that mark a field of possibilities for an emergent Afro-American *national* enterprise. This enterprise (which has been an immanent object of African desire since the Jamestown landing of "twenty negres" in 1619) can be fittingly characterized as the establishment of a mode of *sounding* reality that is identifiably and self-consciously black and empowering. Attempting to answer the question, What, then, is the Negro, this new man?—an inquiry that takes effect only through willed faith in black national possibilities and a corresponding willingness to sound such possibilities—turn-of-the-century spokespersons demonstrated amazing capacities. For they had not only to filter the absurd noises of minstrelsy but also, and at the same instant, to recall sounds of African origin in an age characterized by divided aims, betrayed hopes, and open brutalities. What was required was a shrewd combination of formal mastery and deformative creativity.

If we turn to the Harlem Renaissance of the twenties, it is difficult in the presence of a seminal discursive act like Alain Locke's *New Negro* to conceive of that modern, Afro-American, expressive moment as other than an intensely successful act of national self-definition working itself out in a field of possibilities constructed by turn-of-the-century spokespersons. The title of the book, in its first amazing edition, was *The New Negro: An Interpretation*. This title calls to mind the response that Sterling Brown made to Robert Penn Warren's poetic line, "Nigger, your breed ain't metaphysical." Brown's response: "Cracker, your breed ain't exegetical." Exegesis, hermeneutics, the offices of *interpretation* and fitting analysis vis-à-vis Afro-America, according to Locke's title, are now the project of the black spokesperson him- or herself.

Further, *The New Negro's* dedication to "the younger generation" signals a realization of *change* qualified by *traditional* expressive possibilities. The prose of the dedication is immediately followed by the notation and score of an Afro-American spiritual: "O, rise, shine for Thy Light is a' coming." It is possible to assert, I think, that Locke's editorial work constitutes his song of a new generation, his attempt to provide a singing book of (and for) a new era in Afro-American expressive history.

Surely the space between *The Souls of Black Folk* and *The New Negro*—given the bar from "O, rise, shine for Thy Light is a' coming"—can be thought of as bridged by spiritual sound. It is Locke himself who writes most eloquently of the spirituals in his collection:

> Thematically rich, in idiom of rhythm and harmony richer still, in potentialities of new musical forms and new technical traditions so deep as to be accessible only to genius, they have the respect of the connoisseur even while still under the sentimental and condescending patronage of the amateur.[55]

His most important gesture in regard to the spirituals, however, was his inclusion at virtually the midpoint of his anthology of two songs in their full notation and text. Thus at the center of *The New Negro* one hears the classical sound of Afro-America. And this sounding gesture of national significance is not isolated in the context of the collection as a whole. For Locke's entire project is rife with graphic gestures that produce an *interpretation* of the Afro-American unlike any that had preceded *The New Negro* in Afro-American discursive history.

We witness, for example, the illustrations of Winold Reiss and Aaron Douglas that exploit African motifs (masks in particular) to serve as "ancestral" and culturally specific leitmotivs. The work of Reiss and Douglas serves in fact as a kind of graphic, African presence qualifying and surrounding all prose, poetry, and drama in the volume. In addition, we see Reiss's magnificent color portraits of figures such as Locke, Paul Robeson, Jean Toomer, Countee Cullen, Claude McKay, as well as his genre studies in color and black and white of figures such as the "Brown Madonna," "Negro Teachers," and the "Negro Librarian." We also behold in Locke's essay on the "ancestral arts" photographs of African masks and statues from Bushongo, Sudan-Niger, the Ivory Coast, Dahomey, and Congo. There are, as well, reproductions of title pages from rare and venerable books by Africans in the New World and transcriptions (including musical notations) of the actual *telling* of Afro-American lore recorded by Arthur Huff Fauset.

If DuBois's *Souls* is a diorama of the folk conceived in terms of a "problem," Locke's *New Negro* is surely something more extensive. It is, I believe, a broadening and enlargement of the field of traditional Afro-American discursive possibilities. The work has, in effect, the character of a panorama's "unlimited" view, summoning concerns not of a problematical "folk" but rather those of a newly emergent "race" or "nation"—a *national culture*. Locke's effort is no less performative than DuBois's, and it manages to provide a visual, auditory, and, indeed, almost tactile field that offers new national modes of sounding, interpreting, and speaking "the Negro."

This nationalistic mode sounds in the foreword:

> The New Negro must be seen in the perspective of a New World, and especially of a New America. Europe seething in a dozen centers with emergent nationalities, Palestine full of a renascent Judaism—these are no more alive with the progressive forces of our era than the quickened centers of the lives of black folk. America seeking a new spiritual expansion and artistic maturity, trying to found an American literature, a national art, and a national music implies a Negro-American culture seeking the same satisfactions and objectives. [Pp. xv–xvi]

The world envisioned by *The New Negro*, then, is not one of southern country districts, nor "darkened ghetto[s] of a segregated race life" (p. xvi). Nor does it remotely resemble the universe of minstrel nonsense.

Indeed, the world projected by Locke's collection is a nation comprised of self-consciously aspiring individuals who view their efforts as coextensive with global strivings for self-determination and national cultural expression. One of the strongest statements of this projection occurs in the work's introduction:

> Hitherto, it must be admitted that American Negroes have been a race more in name than in fact, or to be exact, more in sentiment than in experience. The chief bond between them has been that of a common condition rather than a common consciousness; a problem in common rather than a life in common. In Harlem, Negro life is seizing upon its first chances for group expression and self-determination. It is—or promises at least to be—a race capital. That is why our comparison is taken with those nascent centers of folk-expression and self-determination which are playing a creative part in the world today. Without pretense to their political significance, Harlem has the same role to play for the New Negro as

Dublin has had for the New Ireland or Prague for the
New Czechoslovakia. [P. 7]

Not a "problem" but a NATION—this is indeed what
might be considered the extraordinary departure. In an
American era populated by Tom Buchanans in the upper
echelon, Theodore Bilbo and Woodrow Wilson in local and
national politics, Lothrop Stoddard and William Graham
Sumner in scholarship, Octavus Roy Cohen in popular me-
dia, and Snopeses everywhere, Locke's discursive act was
veritably one of *extreme deformation*—of what I want to call
here (and explain fully in a moment) *radical marronage*. We
need but listen to the historian C. Vann Woodward describ-
ing the postwar years in order to gain a reasoned perspective
on the enormous magnitude of *The New Negro's* flight from
the common racialist ground of its era. Woodward writes:

> In the postwar era there were new indications that the
> Southern Way was spreading as the American Way in
> race relations. The great migration of Negroes into the
> residential slum areas and the industrial plants of the big
> Northern cities increased tension between races. North-
> ern labor was jealous of its status and resentful of the
> competition of Negroes, who were excluded from
> unions. Negroes were pushed out of the more desirable
> jobs in industries that they had succeeded in invading
> during the manpower shortage of the war years. They
> were squeezed out of federal employment more and
> more. Negro postmen began to disappear from the old
> routes, as Negro policemen did from their old beats.
> They began to lose their grip upon crafts such as that of
> the barbers, which had once been a virtual monopoly in
> the South.[56]

The historian J. Saunders Redding also offers a bleak
picture of the black situation during the first three decades
of the twentieth century in *They Came in Chains*, noting that
some two million blacks fled the South's disfranchisement,
lynchings, crop failures, and general miseries in a mere five

years during the second decade.[57] It is difficult to conceive of the horribleness of the American scene for black people during the era in which Locke produced his classic collection. But it seems fair to say that patent nonsense and murderous exclusion (lynching statistics rose significantly in an atmosphere of racist, postwar hysteria) were the two most common responses in a United States that adopted Jim Crow, either de facto or de jure, as the law of the land.

I want to suggest that what Locke's declaration of a *nation* amounted to was a gesture commensurate with what Richard Price describes in the introduction to *Maroon Societies* as "marronage on the grand scale."[58] Price defines such marronage as "the banding together [of individual fugitives] to create independent communities of their own, [communities] that struck directly at the foundations of the plantation system, presenting military and economic threats that often taxed the colonists to their very limits" (p. 3). Maroon societies as standard features of the American landscape are noted by Herbert Aptheker in "Maroons Within the Present Limits of the United States":

> An ever-present feature of antebellum southern life was the existence of camps of runaway Negro slaves, often called maroons, when they all but established themselves independently on the frontier. These were seriously annoying, for they were sources of insubordination. They offered havens for fugitives, served as bases for marauding expeditions against nearby plantations and, at times, supplied the nucleus of leadership for planned uprisings. [Quoted in Price, p. 151]

The most astute image of the maroon comes from Price's introduction where the figure is characterized as a person not only possessed of the skills and knowledge of a "master culture" but also motivated by a firm understanding of African modes of existence (p. 20). Price's image captures my own sense of the overall effect and ambience of Locke's *New Negro* as a discursive project:

Maroon men [and women] throughout the hemisphere developed extraordinary skills in guerrilla warfare. To the bewilderment of their European enemies, whose rigid and conventional tactics were learned on the open battlefields of Europe, these highly adaptable and mobile warriors took maximum advantage of local environments, striking and withdrawing with great rapidity, making extensive use of ambushes to catch their adversaries in crossfire, fighting only when and where they chose, depending on reliable intelligence networks among nonmaroons (both slave and white settlers), and often communicating by horns. [Pp. 7–8]

The world of *The New Negro* represents a unified community of national interests set in direct opposition to the general economic, political, and theological tenets of a racist land. The work is, in itself, a *communal* project, drawing on resources, talents, sounds, images, rhythms of a marooned society or nation existing on the frontiers or margins of *all* American promise, profit, and modes of production. It thus seeks its inspiration in the very flight, or marronage, to the urban North of millions of black folk.

The Afro-American masses may feel, in Locke's phrase, "only a strange relief and a new vague urge" (p. 4). They may not be "articulate as yet" (p. 7). Moreover, their current condition may compel them to entrust their expressive potential to black spokespersons of a younger generation. Yet Locke is acutely aware that it is the masses—those millions of blacks leaving, departing, engaged in marronage *on a grand scale*—who are at the forefront of what he conceives as a black national emergence: "The clergyman following his errant flock, the physician or lawyer trailing his clients, supply the true clues. In a real sense it is the rank and file who are leading, and the leaders who are following. A transformed and transforming psychology permeates the masses" (p. 7). The "transforming psychology" which Locke extrapolates from the marronage of Afro-American masses has little to do with frightened and unthinking retreat. Rather:

A Maroon Warrior. An illustration from J. G. Stedman's *Narrative of a Five-Years' Expedition against the Revolted Negroes of Surinam* (London, 1796).

The wash and rush of this human tide on the beach line of the northern city centers is to be explained primarily in terms of a new vision of opportunity, of social and economic freedom, of a spirit to seize, even in the face of an extortionate and heavy toll, a chance for the improvement of conditions. With each successive wave of it, the movement of the Negro becomes more and more a mass movement toward the larger and the more democratic chance—in the Negro's case a deliberate flight not only from countryside to city, but from medieval America to modern. [P. 6]

I think one can say without overstatement that Locke's formative propositions in *The New Negro* are essentially deformative in intent. For they remove the Afro-American decisively from "country districts" of the South and cast a black mass movement in terms that sound like the formulations of nineteenth-century Victorian sages. Locke—like a proud Jeremy Bentham or a confident John Stuart Mill—welcomes "Harlem" and its new masses as a sign of an irreversible shift from the medieval to the modern.

Marronage, masses, and modernism come together in a striking, even an aggressive manner in *The New Negro*. For Locke quickly concedes that the *outer* objectives of the life of Afro-America are coextensive with general American ideals. But he also forcefully notes that the *inner* objectives of the Afro-American nation—located in "the very heart of the folk-spirit" (p. xv)—are still in the process of uneasy formation. What these inner objectives constitute is represented, I think, by the drive and force implied by the graphics of the collection with its African masks, and transcribed spirituals, and the energized portrait of a madonna who gives life to succeeding generations as its frontispiece. Simply stated, the inner objective is to found a nation of Afro-Americans on the basis of RACE.

In a world of murderous exclusion, the mass spirit—articulated through the voices of a younger, expressive generation—demands an inversion that converts "a defensive into an offensive position, a handicap into an incentive" (p.

11). In short, the discourse of lordship and bondage, controlled by the master, will be taken up and transmuted—deformed, as it were—by the maroon. "You have confined me to the language of RACE," Locke's mass spirit seems to say, "and I shall convert it into a weapon and creative instrument of massed, *national,* racial will." Relegated by a na-

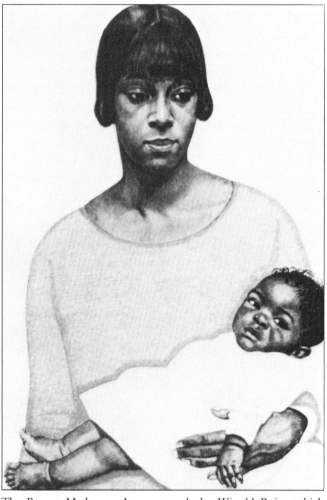

The Brown Madonna. A genre study by Winold Reiss, which serves as frontispiece for *The New Negro* (1925).

tional white consensus to marginality, a position resonant only with *different* expressive possibilities ("and often communicating by horns"), the *New Negro* seeks community and self-consciously pursues democratic advantage through the medium of race.

Words of Richard Wright's narrator in *Black Boy* come to mind: "I did not embrace insurgency through open choice." Similarly, Locke refers to the New Negro's racial/expressive strategy as "forced"; it is a desperate attempt to build "Americanism" on race values (p. 12). But even with its racialistically compelled character, it is *still* insurgency. And Locke knows that only the articulate elite can channel such racially constrained energies in "constructive" ways. He talks of the threat, the danger, the radicalism of the masses represented by such leadership and following as that of Marcus Garvey. Such radicalism can destroy America if a black talented tenth is not allowed to bring about a revaluation of Afro-American expressive culture and communicate with advanced sectors of the white community. The principal metaphor of *The New Negro*'s introduction heightens dramatically one's sense of the work as a deformative act. For that metaphor is of a dammed, blocked, unjustly constrained black current ready to overflow and flood calm plantations beyond marronage. Only a radical change in American polity can forestall this disaster.

The urban masses have thus entered the Afro-American field of possibilities, carrying both leadership force and energetic potential. While Locke's vision is not of a full merger of a formerly distinctive class and mass in Afro-America, it does suggest that the only worthwhile expressive project available to *class* is a national, racial expressivity that takes form and draws heart *only* from the "awakened" Afro-American mass. Further, it suggests that any Afro-American expressive project must find its ultimate validity in a global community—the world, black masses, as it were—of Africans, both continental, and diasporic. Locke knew that guerrilla warfare is always a function of mass and massive support.

9

The radically advanced aspect of *The New Negro* is its inscription of Afro-American modernity in mass, urban, national, and international terms. To achieve this inscription the work appropriates sounding strategies brought to resonant potentiality by turn-of-the-century spokespersons. The collection is in a sense a kind of community of accomplished discursive possibilities. Just as Harlem appears in the work as a sign of marronage and deformation, so Durham, described eloquently by the sociologist E. Franklin Frazier, appears as a sign of formal mastery. If Harlem is, indeed, the "progressive Negro community of the American metropolis" (Locke's phrase, p. xvi) and the veritable national seat of Afro-American intellectual and artistic leadership, then Durham is, in Frazier's piquant phrase, the "Capital of the Black Middle Class" (p. 333). Both city names—one northern, the other southern—stand as tangible emblems, as representations of sounding practices that give birth to Afro-American modernity. Taken together, they give locational form to the projections found at the close of Locke's introduction:

> But whatever the general effect, the present generation
> will have added the motives of self-expression and spir-
> itual development [Harlem] to the old and still un-
> finished task of making material headway and progress
> [Durham]. No one who understandingly faces the situa-
> tion with its substantial accomplishment or views the
> new scene with its still more abundant promise can be
> entirely without hope. [Pp. 15–16]

Indeed, Locke's volume itself provides substantial discursive grounds for hope. His compendium virtually collects, organizes, and gives form to the fullest extensions of a field of sounding possibilities; it serves as both the speaking manual *and* the singing book of a pioneering civilization freed from the burden of nonsensically and polemically constrained expression. Both Paul Kellogg in his essay "Negro Pioneers" and Charles S. Johnson in "The New Frontage on American Life" project a vision of Afro-American settlers bringing into existence what a participant in a seminar I recently conducted called a new American "folk hero"—the "New Negro."[59] Kellogg (a white contributor) sounds this pioneering note as follows:

> In the northward movement of the Negroes in the last ten years, we have another folk migration which in human significance can be compared only with this pushing back of the Western frontier in the first half of the last century or with the waves of immigration which have swept in from overseas in the last half. Indeed, though numerically far smaller than either of these, this folk movement is unique. For this time we have a people singing as they come—breaking through to cultural expression and economic freedom together. [P. 271]

The description of a collective body of people—conjoined in national sentiment and determination—making their way to both the headlands of material success and the peaks of expressive creativity in a single trek is inspiring in the extreme. And what might be called the *institutional* character of their dual achievement (expressive-intellectual as well as material) is projected by Kelly Miller's and Robert R. Moton's respective essays on "Howard: The National Negro University" and "Hampton-Tuskegee: Missioners of the Mass." Like Harlem and Durham, Howard and Hampton-Tuskegee stand as signs of an achieved extension of discursive possibilities first brought forth by DuBois's siting of the *black university* and Washington's delineation of a *black skills center.*

The New Negro, like the valued documents from which we grasp iconic images and pictorial myths of a colonial or frontier America, is perhaps our first *national* book, offering not only a description of streams of tendency in our collective lives but also an actual construction within its pages of the sounds, songs, images, and signs of a nation. The collection's combination of phaneric display and formal mastery can come as no surprise to the person who has followed the lines of Afro-American development through an extensive discursive field. For though the enabling conditions for Locke's collection are found in marronage, there is no gainsaying the work's quite canny presentation, utilization, and praise of formal mastery. Witness, for example, the high evaluation of Countee Cullen's poetry, poetry that is meant to imitate with astute fidelity the efforts of British romanticism. Or turn to Claude McKay's "The White House," a poem whose title Locke changed to "White Houses," and you find an English, or modified Shakespearean, sonnet. Again, most of the short fiction and, certainly, the single drama presented in *The New Negro* scarcely escape initial recognition as formally *standard* works.

The present discussion is hardly the place to explore fully the Afro-American cultural dimensions and significances of McKay's or Cullen's *standard* artistic postures. But one can contextualize such efforts by saying that McKay's "sonnet," like Cullen's "ballads," are just as much mastered *masks* as the minstrel manipulations of Booker T. Washington and Charles Chesnutt are. The trick of McKay and Cullen was what one of my colleagues calls the denigration of form—a necessary ("forced," as it were) adoption of the standard that results in an effective *blackening*.[60] Locke was never of the opinion that Western *standards* in art were anything other than adequate goals for high Afro-American cultural achievement. And the revaluation of the Afro-American based on artistic accomplishment for which he calls mandated, in his view, a willingness on the part of black spokespersons to aspire toward such standards. Hence, one would have to present *recognizably* standard forms and get what black mileage one could out of subtle, or, by contrast, straining (like McKay's rebellious cries) variations and deepenings of these forms. If the younger generation was to proffer "artistic" gifts, such gifts had first to be recognizable as "artistic" by Western, formal standards and not simply as unadorned or primitive *folk* creations.

Now Locke—and, indeed, the entire Harlem movement—has often been criticized severely for its advocacy of the standard. Yet it seems that such criticism proceeds somewhat in ignorance of the full discursive field marking Afro-American national possibilities. For we may not enjoy or find courageous models of derring-do in the masking that characterizes formal mastery, but we certainly cannot minimize its significant and strategic presence in our history. Furthermore, such masking carries subtle resonances and effects that cannot even be perceived (much less evaluated) by the person who begins with the notion that recognizably *standard* form automatically disqualifies a work as an authentic and valuable Afro-American national production. Analysis is in fact foreclosed by a first assumption of failure. Certainly Countee Cullen, for example, served a national need in a time of "forced" institution building and national projection. He gained white American recognition for "Negro poetry" at a moment when there was little encouraging recognition in the United States for *anything* Negro. And Cullen gained such recognition by means of a mastery of form pleasing *to Afro-Americans* as well as Anglo-Americans. It seems inconceivable that, in the first flush of pioneering urbanity and heady self-consciousness, the congregation of Reverend Frederick Cullen's well-attended Salem Methodist Episcopal Church in Harlem would have responded positively if, after the father's announcement of his son's accomplishments as *a poet*, the young Countee had produced sounds such as: "April is the cruellest month, breeding / Lilacs out of the dead land, mixing / Memory and desire, stirring / Dull roots with spring rain." The delivery of such lines would probably have caused consternation akin to the congregation's reaction to John in DuBois's classic story "Of the Coming of John": "Little had they understood of what he said, for he spoke an unknown tongue." Not only was the "tongue" of such collaged allusiveness as Eliot's *unknown* to a congregation like Reverend Cullen's; it was also unnecessary, unneeded, of little use in a world bent on recognizable (rhyme, meter, form, etc.) artistic "contributions." One has only to peruse the 1913 issue of *Poetry* in which Ezra Pound's famous imagist manifesto appeared to see that "cruellest months" and breeding lilacs were the exception rather than the American rule in Cullen's day.

There is no real need to enter apologetics for *The New Negros'* presentation and use of formal mastery, however, since this strategy takes its significance from the entire sounding field of our nation; it is, moreover, dramatically complemented or even *out-sounded* by the deformative iconography and syllables of the collection. This deformation finds resonance in Jean Toomer's intensely lyrical prose-songs of Southern black women and in Cugo Lewis's rendition of the etiological "T'appin." It takes effect in Jessie Fauset's keen signifying on Joel Chandler Harris and all white spokesmen who would make the Negro merely the "funny man" of American life. It expresses itself in the call for a National Black Theatre (Montgomery Gregory), a National Black University (Kelly Miller), and a National School of Negro Art (Locke). But most important, the deformative rhythms, signs, and images of *The New Negro* find their proper curve in the movement of Locke's collection from a reasoned, if heady, statement of Afro-American national ideals to an impassioned delineation by a venerable and formidable Afro-American scholar of the global significance and mission implicit in the achievement of such ideals.

One might say in fact that *The New Negro*—commencing with the figure of 175,000 men and women of color in Harlem—ends with a vision of the mission of Harlem vis-à-vis a global community of Africans 150 million in number.

Alain Locke. Portrait by Winold Reiss, which appeared in
The New Negro (1925).

For the collection concludes with W. E. B. DuBois's "The
Negro Mind Reaches Out."

DuBois's work analyzes world colonialism as a function
of the bizarre and unfortunate alliance of exploitative capital
and derogated labor, suggesting that a murderous white exclusion is the enabling condition for this alliance. Surely,
DuBois's is a phaneric voice when he writes:

The attitude of the white laborer toward colored folk is largely a matter of long continued propaganda and gossip. The white laborers can read and write, but beyond this their education and experience are limited and they live in a world of color prejudice. The curious, most childish propaganda dominates us, by which good, earnest, even intelligent men have come by millions to believe almost religiously that white folk are a peculiar and chosen people whose one great accomplishment is civilization and that civilization must be protected from the rest of the world by cheating, stealing, lying, and murder. [P. 407]

Hope for the future lies in the political reeducation of white workers and in effective leadership for global black masses who suffer the effects of an industrial imperialism unchecked in its greed and brutality. DuBois, of course, designates the seat of leadership for the black masses as the United States:

This hundred and fifty millions of people are gaining slowly an intelligent thoughtful leadership. The main seat of their leadership is to-day the United States. [For] in the United States there are certain unheralded indications of development in the Negro problem. One is the fact that for the first time in America, the American Negro is to-day universally recognized as capable of speaking for himself. [P. 411]

("And often communicating by horns," "and often communicating by horns . . .") The *sound* of DuBois is a challenge to those celebrated at the beginning of *The New Negro*—the younger generation. The collection is not only a national sounding field but also the sounding of an international mission bestowed by venerability upon youth. The maroon community of "Harlem," conceived as the *modern* capital of those "capable of speaking" for themselves, is thus source (of insubordination)—haven (for fugitives)—base (for marauding expeditions)—and nucleus (of leadership for planned uprisings).

10

The ready acknowledgment that *The New Negro* is the first fully modern figuration of a nation predicated upon mass energies returns us to the present discussion's exploration of definitions of Afro-American "modernism." Locke's collection is not, however, the clearest instance of a full discursive engagement *with* such mass energies. Although his work set the stage for such an engagement, the editor left the task itself to a "younger generation": "Youth speaks, and the voice of the New Negro is heard. What stirs inarticulately in the masses is already vocal upon the lips of the talented few, and the future listens, however the present may shut its ears" (p. 47). I want to suggest that a complete expressive modernity was achieved only when the "Harlem Renaissance" gave way to what might be called—following the practices of Anglo-American and British moderns—"renaissancism." By this term, I want to suggest a *spirit* of nationalistic engagement that begins with intellectuals, artists, and spokespersons at the turn of the century and receives extensive definition and expression during the 1920s. This spirit is one that prompts the black artist's awareness that his or her only possible foundation for authentic and modern expressivity resides in a discursive field marked by formal mastery and sounding deformation. Further, I want to suggest that "renaissancism" connotes something quite removed from a single, exotic set of "failed" high jinks confined to less than a decade. It signals in fact a resonantly and continuously productive set of tactics, strategies, and syllables that takes form at the turn of the century and extends to our own day. One of the most obvious cullings of renaissancism's fruits occurs in the thirties and situates itself firmly in accord with deformative possibilities inherent in *The New Negros'* validation of the folk, or, the vernacular.

Gone in the work of a poet like Sterling Brown is the felt necessity to produce only *recognizably* standard forms. What replaces this drive is an unashamed and bold dedication (a dedication that remains, for the most part, implicit in the sotto voce urgings of the Harlem 1920s) to rendering the actual folk voice in its simple, performative eloquence. If a black, folk, national voice existed, the thirties seemed to realize that it was not far to seek. Gertrude "Ma" Rainey, Bessie Smith, Mamie Smith, Victoria Spivey, Ida Cox, Alberta Hunter, Sleepy John Estes, Barbecue Bob, Robert Johnson, Blind Boy Fuller, Big Bill Broonzy, and other vernacular singers from the "New Orleans Delta on down" had taken the United States—and the Afro-American masses—by storm.

Similarly, spirituals and jazz, Afro-American "terribleness" and flair had received rave reviews and serious attention from a second decade white population somehow "desolate and sick of an old passion." Blues releases sold by the tens of thousands in the 1920s, and the folk energy and achievement that they represented gained global recognition for what can only be called a black and classical sound of the self-in-marronage.[61] A college-bred black man like Sterling Brown, standing as a member of a second (or even a third) twentieth-century Afro-American intellectual generation, could readily set himself the task of knowing the score where the folk national (blues) voice was concerned. The inroads on myths and shibboleths, nonsense and exclusion, made by a first (and perhaps second) generation ensured Brown the necessary emotional and intellectual confidence to mine a southern Afro-American tradition with dedicated genius.

The indisputably modern moment in Afro-American discourse arrives, I believe, when the *intellectual* poet Brown,

92

masterfully mantled in the wisdom of his Williams College Phi Beta Kappa education, gives forth the deformative sounds of Ma Rainey. (The actual meeting between the poet and Ma Rainey occurred in Nashville in 1928, at a Cedar Street theater.[62] The musicologist John Work provided what today must seem a fitting third in this historic encounter.) The blending, I want to suggest, of class and mass—*poetic* mastery discovered as a function of deformative *folk* sound—constitutes the essence of black discursive modernism. This blend is achieved within a fluid field. Indeed, if you have ever heard the blues righteously sung, you know that it sounds of and from fields burning under torpid Southern suns, or lands desolately drenched by too high rivers. The intended audience is black people themselves defined by the very blues tones and lyrics as sharers in a nation of common concern and culturally specific voice.

Renaissancism's success consists in a fruitfully resounding merger. We listen as what the critic Stephen Henderson[63] calls a religious rite and cultural performance takes place in the soundings of Sterling Brown:

Ma Rainey

I

When Ma Rainey
Comes to town,
Folks from anyplace
Miles aroun',
From Cape Girardeau,
Poplar Bluff,
Flocks in to hear
Ma do her stuff;
Comes flivverin' in,
Or ridin' mules,
Or packed in trains,
Picknickin' fools. . . .
That's what it's like,
Fo' miles on down,
To New Orleans delta
An' Mobile town,

When Ma hits
Anywheres aroun'.

II

Dey comes to hear Ma Rainey from de little river
    settlements,
From blackbottom cornrows and from lumber camps;
Dey stumble in de hall, jes a-laughin' an'a-cacklin',
Cheerin' lak roarin' water, lak wind in river swamps.
An' some jokers keeps deir laughs a-goin' in de crowded
    aisles,
An' some folks sits dere waitin' wid deir aches an'
    miseries,
Till Ma comes out before dem, a-smilin' gold-toofed
    smiles
An' Long Boy ripples minors on de black an' yellow
    keys.

III

O Ma Rainey,
Sing yo' song;
Now you's back
Whah you belong,
Git way inside us,
Keep us strong. . . .
O Ma Rainey,
Li'l an' low;
Sing us 'bout de hard luck
Roun' our do';
Sing us 'bout de lonesome road
We mus' go. . . .

IV

I talked to a fellow, an' the fellow say,
"She jes' catch hold of us, somekindaway.
She sang Backwater Blues one day:
    'It rained fo' days an' de skies was dark as night,
    Trouble taken place in de lowlands at night.
    'Thundered an' lightened an' the storm begin to roll
    Thousan's of people ain't got no place to go.
    'Den I went an' stood upon some high ol' lonesome hill,
    An' looked down on the place where I used to live.'

An' den de folks, dey natchally bowed dey heads an'
   cried,
Bowed dey heavy heads, shet dey moufs up tight an'
   cried,
An' Ma lef' de stage, an' followed some de folks
   outside."

Dere wasn't much more de fellow say:
She jes' gits hold of us dataway.[64]

And, indeed, after hearing a Sterling Brown performance of
"Ma Rainey" there is not much a fellow can say, except perhaps that Zora Neale Hurston and Richard Wright move to
the same rhythms witnessed in Brown's ritual. Or perhaps
that Brown's discursive gesture implies that the modernity
and effectiveness of Afro-American expression always summon to view and to audition black sufferers of marginaliza-
tion and dispossession. The image of renaissancism par
excellence is a mass image. It stands opposed to an economics of slavery that has always attempted to figure us as the
mindlessly deformed, fit only for brutal servitude.
   Renaissancism not only summons a mass image but converts it into a salvific sound that becomes a spirit house and
space of black habitation. For the very sufferers imaged are a
people of will and strength who convert *marronage* into
song, story, arts of liberation, and guerrilla war. There is
quite frequently among them a communicating by horns.
And their image translates at last into the mask of a resounding and venerable ancestry of fields. The task of the spokesperson who would engage the sound of folk conversion is to
situate himself or herself in productive relationship to a field
marked by awesome strategies of deformation and mastery.
It is this discursive field that links us bone of the bone, flesh
of the flesh, and note by resounding blue note to contours
of those transforming African masks that constitute our
beginnings.
   Perhaps all of this is implicit in the statement by Marcus
Garvey that Professor Robert Hill was kind enough to share

Gertrude "Ma" Rainey. (Courtesy of the Moorland-Spingarn Research Center, Howard University.)

with me.[65] In one of his Liberty Hall speeches, the indefatigable leader of the 1920s warned opponents that he could not be tampered with or harmed because, as he said, "I am a *modern*." And if we of the present generation comprehend the success constituted by Harlem's production of a tome such as *The New Negro* and are happily successful in our own

An Afro-American family dwelling photographed in Caroline County, Virginia, during the 1940s.

renaissancism, we may share the confidence, indeed, the critical invulnerability claimed by Garvey. *The New Negro* constitutes a national reference point and treasure that will be summoned (perhaps "by horns") whenever there is a genuinely national surge among us, or whenever we reflect on our mission of African liberation, or whenever we acknowledge, in bold terms, that the massed folk are rank and file leaders of any group movement forward that we might make. It is no surprise that 1955 witnessed the publication at Howard University of Rayford Logan's collection dedicated to Alain Locke and entitled *The New Negro Thirty Years Afterward,* nor is it uncanny that Afro-American cultural nationalism and radical activism of the 1960s and 1970s styled itself "Renaissance II."

11

Black preachers enjoin neophytes to conclude by "tellin' 'em what you *have* said." I have said previously and wish now to reiterate that my aim is not reductionism. I do not want to imply that a twofold categorization of variables such as the mastery of form and the deformation of mastery occasions a simple duality. The dynamics of these strategies can be captured analogically by a rectangular-coordinate graph, a Cartesian plane, or a symmetrical (normal) distribution. In a Cartesian coordinate system, any point positioned relative to horizontal and vertical axes implies all other possible points. The single point thus suggests a fluid field of possibilities. Any instance of the mastery of form is always suggestive of its deformative correspondent and vice versa. If a perfect blend of mastery and deformation is considered the mean, then the discursive field of Afro-American modernism can accurately be conceived as a symmetrical distribution. The complex fluidity of Booker T. Washington's "speaking manual" (which is as fine a description of *Up from Slavery* as I can provide) illustrates, as I sought to demonstrate earlier, a black discursive field. For by talking of subversion and the spirituals and the revolutionary fervor with which Afro-Americans changed their names after emancipation, Washington shows in the very opening pages of his narrative that he is cognizant of strategies of deformation. At the same time, he demonstrates that he knows that it is a minstrel mask he must master if he wishes to advance a Tuskegee project.

Similarly, W. E. B. DuBois makes masterful appeals to

the "best" whites in order to forward his deformative university project. Sterling Brown—in a gesture that implies self-conscious evolutionism in craftsmanship (and, one suspects, a masterful black "craftiness" as well)—entitles the last section of his vernacular *Southern Road* "Vestiges." He fills the section with standard poems such as *"Nous n'irons plus au bois."* Richard Wright, in a 1945 deconstruction of the very premises on which a masterful LITERATURE rests, adopted a Western form par excellence as his recognizably standard vehicle. His *Black Boy* is advertised as autobiography—as, in fact, "A Record of Childhood and Youth." The advertisement as subtitle provides wonderfully innocent camouflage for a work that, as I have detailed in a recent study, employs carnivalesque discourse and zero-degree writing to present a blues world and to sound, in the process, an insurgently blue note of *marronage*.[66]

Afro-American expressive culture appears in its complex continuity and genuine cultural authenticity when it is analyzed according to the model that I have proposed in my foregoing discussions. "Authenticity" is a sign that can connote powers of certification and invoke a world of rarefied connoisseurship—and a desire, as well, for only the genuine and the original. What I intend by the term, however, is not a *raffiné* ARTWORLD projected by institutional theories of expression, but rather an everyday world occupied by our grand, great-grand, and immediate parents—our traceable ancestry that judged certain select sounds appealing and considered them efficacious in the office of a liberating advancement of THE RACE.

To invoke a personal note, I call the name of my father who died in 1983, but who, for the seventy-five active years that he worked in America, moved to the cadences of *Up from Slavery*. His earliest parental instructions became recognizable to me as Washingtonian formulas only when I taught the Tuskegee orator's work during the late 1960s. Only during the past year and a half have I come to understand and appreciate Washington's memorable, remembered, and re-membering legacy of sound to black generations. Ask my in-laws what DuBois said, wrote, or accomplished (neither my mother-in-law nor father-in-law, both of whom are quite brilliant, had the luxury of a college education), and they will draw a blank. But let Washington's name appear, and their eyes glow. They remember, and are re-membered by his oratorical promise of American reward for Negro merit, by the tangible monument he built at Tuskegee. Or there is my New York uncle who commented on the housecleaning that I was doing (at age twelve) to earn my allowance: "When you finish, I am going to take a handkerchief and go over your work like Booker T. Washington's boss. Do you know that story?"

Storied SOUNDS that have come through my lineage (like the adage that one can always locate the black section of an American city by checking the directory for "Booker T. Washington High School," extended today, of course, to include "Martin Luther King School") speak to the importance of a sounding mastery of form in Afro-American life. The prevalence and importance of strategies of mastery are not difficult to discover. For any behavior that is designated "modernist" for Afro-America is also, and by dint of adequate historical accounts, always, coextensively labeled popular, economic, and liberating. What exists on the antecedent side of black modernity is not a line of stodgy, querulous, and resistant premoderns but a universe of enslavement. In the slave world, discourse was figured not as, say, repressed Victorian or Puritan formulas, but as hard won song and courageously expostulated black oratory (and written prose) designed to move the spirit of freedom. Modernist "anxiety" in Afro-American culture does not stem from a fear of replicating outmoded forms or of giving way to bourgeois formalisms. Instead, the anxiety of modernist influence is produced, in the first instance, by the black spokesperson's necessary task of employing audible extant forms in ways that move clearly *up*, masterfully and re-soundingly away from slavery.

For the modern black spokesperson, to *re-sound* African interests invested in black song and in the black abolitionist discourse produced in America from 1619 to, say, 1895, by mastering the available mask of minstrelsy was to open a field not only of discursive possibilities but also of radically altered black life choices. Speech, talk, *sounds* of wage labor and gainful employment were radically modern against a backdrop of exploitative impoverishment and barbarous enslavement. "I found employment," writes Frederick Douglass of his activities as a fugitive slave (a maroon) in New Bedford,

> the third day after my arrival, in stowing a sloop with a load of oil. It was new, dirty, and hard work for me; but I went at it with a glad heart and a willing hand. I was now my own master. It was a happy moment, the rapture of which can be understood only by those who have been slaves. It was the first work, the reward of which was to be entirely my own. There was no Master Hugh standing ready, the moment I earned the money, to rob me of it.[67]

"Entirely my own" captures the sense of "authenticity" that resonates through recognizable masks and standard forms mastered by modern Afro-American spokespersons. (In the passage cited, for example, Douglass's self-in-marronage is masterfully disguised as the earnest face of free enterprise. The black fugitive plays entrepreneur.) Washington—like my father—never believed for an instant that white men and women were anything other than temporarily empowered exploiters who could be masterfully spoken out of money—money that might, in turn, be used to build a free, black nation on the ruins of a slavery the exploiters had maliciously instituted and malevolently maintained. (My father managed to conduct a successful million-dollar campaign—a good deal of the money coming from white philanthropists—in a racialist Louisville, Kentucky, in order to build that city's first black hospital.)

In the camp (or vale) of deformation, DuBois also understood that the formative options of blacks were, at least, a function of white finance. This became abundantly clear to him when he was compelled to resign his academic post at Atlanta University because his sounding on Washington resulted in the withdrawal of white philanthropy (which far preferred Tuskegee mastery to Atlanta phaneric display). Having seen the writing on the wall, DuBois wrote in 1910: "I insist on my right to think and speak; but if that freedom is made an excuse for abuse of and denial of aid to Atlanta University, then with regret I shall withdraw from Atlanta University."[68] Withdraw he did.

Modernism, then, consists also in a forced movement and northern marronage (Douglass in New Bedford, DuBois at NAACP and Crisis headquarters in New York, Wright in southside Chicago hovels) where a word, a speech distinguishable in kind from Washington's, finds an economic support different in kind from that bestowed on Tuskegee. I want to suggest that this support is internal (*within* the maroon community itself, in the *yard* of the Caribbean, the black urban enclave of the United States, or the tribal compound of African forests) and fosters the deformation of mastery. Perhaps the appropriate signs here are "tribal," "ancestral," and "racial" in combination with "spiritual" and "wisdom."

We know that infant gorillas display the chest-thumping behavior of phaneric resolution. Similarly, I hear ancestral injunctions as clearly at this moment as in my distant youthful days in a wretchedly poor community in Louisville, where many homes lacked plumbing and electricity, but where black bottom boogies, fish fries, frenzied churchgoing, and furiously loving folks held their own. I hear my father saying, "Son, the only time you have my complete permission to punch a man in the face is if he calls you 'Nigger.'" Sonia Sanchez—from deep-Alabama roots—remembers this same sound of marooned black childhood as "Don't never let *nobody* hit you more than once."[69] Support for the deformation of mastery implies an altered definition of economics. Or, perhaps, it suggests the *ur*-definition insofar as the discipline of economics is the study of human wants and their satisfaction. As a science of desire, perhaps the economics of deformation are the coding of African, tribal, or racial sounds as active, outgoing resistance and response to oppressive ignorance and silencing. The valued act, the best interest of the sui generis and communal group, is judged by such economics as the forwarding and protection of an African sound even if the entailments include violence and death. Don L. Lee (now Haki Madhubuti) and John Coltrane sounds illustrate the point in "Don't Cry, Scream":

> SCREAMMMM/we-eeeee/screech/tee improvise
> aheeeeeeeee/screeeeee/theeee/ee with
> ahHHHHHHHHH/WEEEEEEEE/scrEEE feeling
>   EEEE
> we-eeeeee WE-EEEEEEEEEEEE-EE-EEEEE
> the ofays heard you &
> were wiped out. spaced.
> one clown asked me during,
> *my favorite things,* if
> you were practicing.
> i fired on the muthafucka & said,
> "i'm practicing."[70]

"Don't never let *nobody* hit you more than once."

W. E. B. DuBois is, perhaps, not as well-known to my in-laws as Washington because DuBois never became a public figure in the economics that supported Tuskegee. But it is dead certain that my North Carolina father-in-law, who sat up nights during tobacco-curing season with a brick in his hand (if the brick dropped, you knew you had become too drowsy and were not paying proper attention to the curing) knows and heeds DuBois's inner-tribal, ancestral, and folk-fighting strategies and would never let nobody jump on his sounds more than once.

My tale, then, to say again what I have said, is of a com-

The author's family. Top left: Joseph C. Pierce, Sr. Top right: the author; his wife, Charlotte Pierce Baker; and their son, Mark Frederick. Bottom left: Houston A. Baker, Sr. Bottom right: Grandparents Elizabeth and John Smith; the author (left) and his brothers William and John.

plex field of sounding strategies in Afro-America that are part of a family. The family's history always—no matter how it is revised, purified, distorted, or emended—begins in an economics of slavery. The modernity of our family's sounding strategies resides in their deployment for economic (whether to ameliorate desire or to secure material advantage) advancement. The metaphor that I used earlier seems more than apt for such salvific soundings—they are, indeed, *blues geographies* that can never be understood outside a family commitment. In order to ride the moving blinds on up the road in such territories, it is necessary not only to ask your mama but also to understand fully the sweet renaissancism in even her most standardized songs, as well as in her late-night blues. Harlem is but a moment in such renaissancism, as Langston Hughes recognized—a moment between McKay's arrival from Jamaica and the day in the late 1930s when Hughes introduced his friend Richard Wright to a newly arrived Ralph Ellison (who still lives uptown).[71] Zora Neale Hurston's departing blues coda might have been read by all three men as a sounding bridge between that moment in the thirties and our day: "Been here and gone."

The family signature is always a renewing renaissancism that ensures generation, generations, the mastery of form and the deformation of mastery. What I *have* said is that the family *must* explore its own geographies by transcending an old economics where the familiar signs are LITERATURE, ART, and particularly and most expressly FAILURE. Renaissancism's contemporary fate is our responsibility, demanding a hard and ofttimes painful journey back to ancestral wisdom in order to achieve a traditional (family) goal. That goal is the discovery of our *successful* voices as the always already blues script—as the salvific changing same—in which a new world's future will be sounded. Our modernism consists, finally, not in tumbling towers or bursts in the violet air, but in a sounding renaissancism where a blues reason may yet prevail:

> Well the sun's gonna shine in my back door some day,
> Oh yes, the sun, sun's gonna shine in my back door
>   some day,
> Wind's gonna rise and blow my blues away.

If the spokespersons and other productive black men and women of 1920s' Harlem are auditioned in relation to a sounding field called *renaissancism,* their contribution and value as national resources and as audible signs of the human will's resistance to tyranny and the human mind's masterful and insistent engagement with forms and deformation can only be judged a resounding success. The possibility of such analysis and study and the optimistic results they augur are the real end of what I have said.

Notes

1. Versions of the following essay were prepared and delivered as lectures for the English Institute (August 1985) and the Afro-American Studies department at Yale University (November 1985). At the Institute, I coordinated a panel on modernism and Afro-American literature. At Yale, I had the privilege of delivering the Richard Wright Lecture.

2. Harry Levin, "What Was Modernism?" *Massachusetts Review* 1 (Aug. 1960): 630.

3. Robert Martin Adams, "What Was Modernism?" *Hudson Review* 31 (Spring 1978): 31–32.

4. "POSTmodernISM: A Paracritical Bibliography," *New Literary History* 3 (Autumn 1971): 7.

5. T. S. Eliot, "The Waste Land," in *Modern Poetry*, ed. Maynard Mack et al., 2d ed. (Englewood Cliffs, N.J.: Prentice-Hall, 1961), pp. 157–58.

6. F. Scott Fitzgerald, *The Great Gatsby* (New York: Scribner's 1953), p. 13.

7. See Lionel Trilling, "On the Teaching of Modern Literature," in *Beyond Culture: Essays on Literature and Learning* (New York: Harcourt Brace, 1965), pp. 3–27.

8. Fitzgerald, *The Great Gatsby*, p. 69.

9. I refer, of course, to Conrad's "Heart of Darkness."

10. D. H. Lawrence, *Women in Love* (New York: Viking, 1974).

11. The reference is to *The Emperor Jones*.

12. Trilling, "On the Teaching of Modern Literature," pp. 7–8.

13. Wystan Hugh Auden's ordinary citizen as "Modern Man" is coldly described by the speaker of "The Citizen (To JS/07/M/378 This marble Monument Is Erected by the State)," a 1940 poem: "in the modern sense of an old-fashioned word, he was a saint" (*Modern Poetry*, ed. Mack, p. 206). The speaker is not undone when his/her report is broken by someone's question about such exemplary conduct: "Was he free? Was he happy?" The speaker an-

swers: "The Question is absurd: / Had anything been wrong, we should certainly have heard."

14. In *Madness and Civilization*, Michel Foucault argues that it is de rigueur for a rational, bourgeois, capitalist state to "confine" the poor, the criminal, and the insane in order to know the boundaries of affluence, sanity, and innocence. It is, however, *confinement* in itself that enforces the categories; if you are an inmate of a "total institution" (like a prison, or, American slavery as the "prisonhouse of bondage"), then you are automatically classified according to the defining standards of that institution. The Kantian reference is, of course, to the *Critique of Judgment* (1790). Once "ART" and "AESTHETICS" are distinguished from "popular culture" and "low taste," then one has effected a confinement that can be enforced merely by mentioning a word. Such distinctions—resting on Western metaphysics—can be used to defend and preserve canons of literature and to protect "artistic" masterpieces from all criticism. Only "*men* of taste" are held to possess the developed "aesthetic sense" and sensibility requisite to identification and judgment of genuine works of ART. If such men declare that a product is *not* ART but a product of some other category, there is no escape from their authority of confinement—except subversion.

15. James Weldon Johnson, "Foreword," *Challenge* 1 (1934): 1.

16. Nathan Huggins, *Harlem Renaissance* (New York: Oxford University Press, 1971), p. 309.

17. David Levering Lewis, *When Harlem Was in Vogue* (New York: Alfred A. Knopf, 1981), p. 117. The phrase "when Harlem was in vogue" is drawn from the section of Langston Hughes's autobiography *The Big Sea* (1940) devoted to the Harlem Renaissance. Hughes writes of the renaissance as a mere "vogue" set in motion and largely financed by white downtowners while Negroes played minstrel and trickster roles in it all. A time of low seriousness and charming highjinks is what Hughes (one hopes ironically) portrays. In fact, I think Hughes' characterization is as much a product of the dreadful disappointment he suffered when his patron (Mrs. R. Osgood Mason) dumped him because he decided to write an "engaged" poem, a "socialist" response to the opening of a luxury hotel in New York when so many were starving. He reads treacherous patronage over the entire Harlem Renaissance. Further, to say, as Hughes does, that you were "only funning" is to dampen the pain that results if *you* were really serious and your patron was "funning" all along. In any case, I believe Hughes's account (partially because he lived and produced wonderful work

through subsequent generations) has had an enormous effect on subsequent accounts of the renaissance.

18. Ibid., pp. 305–6.

19. Quoted in George Rochberg, "The Avant-Garde and the Aesthetics of Survival," *New Literary History* 3 (Autumn 1971): 75.

20. See Amiri Baraka (LeRoi Jones), *Black Music* (New York: William Morrow, 1967).

21. Booker T. Washington, *Up from Slavery*, in *Three Negro Classics,* ed. John Hope Franklin (New York: Avon, 1969), p. 140. All citations to Washington's work refer to this edition and are hereafter marked by page numbers in parentheses.

22. The critic Henry Louis Gates, Jr. has produced an intriguing essay on masking and dialect in Afro-American expressive traditions. As in the past, I find myself in accord with his speculations. The essay is entitled "Dis and Dat: Dialect and the Descent" and appears in *Afro-American Literature: The Reconstruction of Instruction,* ed. Dexter Fisher and Robert B. Stepto (New York: Modern Language Association, 1978), pp. 88–119.

23. Constance Rourke, *The Roots of American Culture and Other Essays* (New York: Harcourt Brace, 1942), pp. 269–70. The essay in which the passage appears is entitled "Traditions for a Negro Literature."

24. William Melvin Kelley, *A Different Drummer* (New York: Avon, 1969), pp. 195–96.

25. Susan Stewart, *Nonsense: Aspects of Intertexuality in Folklore and Literature* (Baltimore: Johns Hopkins University Press, 1978), pp. 186–87.

26. Quoted from J. L. Dillard, *Black English: Its History and Usage in the United States* (New York: Random House, 1972), p. 92. The earlier quotation from a minstrel show oration appears in Charles Townsend, *Negro Minstrels* (Upper Saddle River, N.J.: Literature House/Greg Press, 1969), p. 56.

27. Harriet Beecher Stowe, *Uncle Tom's Cabin* (New York: Collier, 1967), p. 256.

28. Ibid., pp. 294–95.

29. Ralph Ellison, *Invisible Man* (New York: Random House, 1952). The words are part of the first chapter of the novel and are important white code phrases for the classification of the protagonist and his peers in the "Battle Royal" scene and in the later Brotherhood scene in which the protagonist delivers a fiery speech in a boxing arena.

30. The names of Kersands, Williams, and Walker are those of

black men who possessed enormous theatrical talent (Williams was in fact a genius of pantomime and comedy) but who found themselves with but one role to play on an American stage—that of minstrelsy. Converting confinement into the birth of genius, they effectively subverted minstrelsy through their original and energetic "plays" within the form. For an account of these performers, see Langston Hughes and Milton Meltzer, *Black Magic: A Pictorial History of the Negro in American Entertainment* (Englewood Cliffs, N.J.: Prentice-Hall, 1967).

31. An account of the correspondence appears in Helen M. Chesnutt's *Charles Waddell Chesnutt: Pioneer of the Color Line* (Chapel Hill: University of North Carolina Press, 1952), p. 241. All further references to Chesnutt's correspondence, marked by page numbers in parentheses, are to this volume.

32. Paul Laurence Dunbar, "The Poet," *Complete Poems* (New York: Dodd, Mead, 1913), p. 191. I have quoted from the Apollo Edition. All subsequent references to Dunbar's poetry, marked by page numbers in parentheses, refer to this paperback edition.

33. James Weldon Johnson, ed., *The Book of American Negro Poetry* (New York: Harcourt, Brace, 1922). I have employed the paperback in which the "Preface to the First Edition" covers pp. 9–48. The Dunbar quote appears on pp. 35–36.

34. Ibid., p. 36.

35. Charles Waddell Chesnutt, *The Conjure Woman* (Ann Arbor: University of Michigan Press, 1969), pp. 163–64. All subsequent references to Chesnutt's collection are marked by page numbers in parentheses.

36. H. B. Cott, "Animal Form in Relation to Appearance," in *Aspects of Form: A Symposium on Form in Art and Nature*, ed. Lancelot Law Whyte (Bloomington: Indiana University Press, 1951), p. 122.

37. Ibid., p. 123.

38. Colin Groves, *Gorillas* (New York: Arco, 1970), pp. 38–39.

39. Olaudah Equiano, *The Life of Olaudah Equiano, or, Gustavus Vassa, the African*, in *Great Slave Narratives*, ed. Arna Bontemps (Boston: Beacon Press, 1969), p. 5, my emphasis; W. E. B. DuBois, *The Souls of Black Folk*, in *Three Negro Classics*, p. 209.

40. William Shakespeare, *The Tempest*, act 1, sc. 2, ll. 365–67; all further references to this work will be included in the text.

41. Ralph Waldo Emerson, "Nature," in *American Poetry and Prose* ed. Norman Foerster (Boston: Houghton Mifflin, 1962), p. 467.

42. Ibid., p. 467.

43. For a discussion of Lamming's perspective, see Janheinz Jahn, *Neo-African Literature: A History of Black Writing* (New York: Grove, 1969), p. 240. Jahn's own perspective adds considerable interest to the Calibanistic problematic. For a discussion of this problematic in relationship to Afro-American slave narratives, see my own discussion, "Autobiographical Acts and the Voice of the Southern Slave," in my work *The Journey Back: Issues in Black Literature and Criticism* (Chicago: University of Chicago Press, 1980).

44. James Baldwin, *Notes of a Native Son* (Boston: Beacon, 1962), p. 6. *Notes* appeared originally in 1955.

45. Jacques Derrida, *Of Grammatology*, trans. Gayatri Chakravorty Spivak (Baltimore: Johns Hopkins University Press, 1976), p. 52.

46. One of the very finest discussions of *Souls*, including this observation on the plurality of the word, greatly influenced my analysis of the work in the present essay. That discussion appears in Arnold Rampersad, *The Art and Imagination of W. E. B. DuBois* (Cambridge, Mass.: Harvard University Press, 1976).

47. DuBois, *The Souls of Black Folk*, in *Three Negro Classics*, p. 387. All further references to *Souls* refer to this edition and are marked by page numbers in parentheses.

48. The phrase, of course, appears in *Cahier d'un retour au pays natal* as a sign for pretechnological societies like the poet's own Martinique.

49. The line was delivered in a Sunday afternoon church performance in New York, and I am indebted to Professor Eleanor Traylor (who was present) for the anecdote.

50. See "The Black Man of Culture," in *Long Black Song* (Charlottesville: University Press of Virginia, 1972).

51. Professor Benston was kind enough to speak on "cultural performance" in relationship to the specific form of the chant sermon and the general concerns of Afro-American expressive modernism during a Summer Seminar for College Teachers supported by the National Endowment for the Humanities that I conducted in 1985. Professor Benston's comments combined with the extraordinarily helpful comments of participants in the seminar to aid me in exploring issues of Afro-American modernism. I am very grateful to all concerned.

52. Dunbar, *The Sport of the Gods* (New York: Arno Press, 1969), p. 1.

53. See *Blues, Ideology, and Afro-American Literature: A Vernacular Theory* (Chicago: University of Chicago Press, 1984).

54. The word "bookooing" is defined in Zora Neale Hurston's *Mules and Men* (1935) as "loud talking, bullying, woofing. From French *beaucoup.*" Reed is a master of the form.

55. Alain Locke, ed., *The New Negro* (New York: Atheneum, 1968), p. 200. All citations to essays in this collection refer to this edition and are hereafter marked by page numbers in parentheses.

56. C. Vann Woodward, *The Strange Career of Jim Crow* (New York: Oxford University Press, 1968), p. 115.

57. See J. Saunders Redding, *They Came in Chains* (New York: Lippincott, 1950), p. 235.

58. Richard Price, ed., *Maroon Societies: Rebel Slave Communities in the Americas* (Baltimore: Johns Hopkins University Press, 1979), p. 3. All citations refer to this edition.

59. See note 51. The observation came from Professor Carolyn Liston.

60. The note on *denigration* comes from my former student, Professor Michael Awkward, who has constructed his own quite provocative model of black discursive practices vis-à-vis Afro-American women writers.

61. The sign "self-in-marronage" comes from the work of Edward Braithwaite of Jamaica who has produced his own study of the phenomenon of marronage in the Caribbean. I encountered the term most recently in a study by Gordon Rohlehr entitled "Articulating a Caribbean Aesthetic." The paper was a handout at a lecture on Calypso presented by Professor Rohlehr at the University of Pennsylvania on 25 November 1985. What the term seems to imply is the always already AFRICAN SELF that has its being in community and cultural/racial/tribal interiority.

62. I am indebted to two people for information on the encounter between Brown and Ma Rainey—Eleanor Jones Baker, my sister-in-law, who first brought the matter to my attention, and Professor Joanne V. Gabbin, Brown's biographer, who went to the source to confirm my sister-in-law's memory that she had read about such an encounter during her research on minstrelsy. "How did you find the information?" I asked Professor Gabbin. "I called Sterling up and asked him," she responded. My gratitude.

63. See Stephen E. Henderson, "The Heavy Blues of Sterling Brown: A Study of Craft and Tradition," *Black American Literature Forum* 14 (Spring 1980): 32–44.

64. *The Collected Poems of Sterling A. Brown,* selected by Michael S. Harper (New York: Harper, 1980), pp. 62–63.

65. Professor Hill wrote of his own interest in black modernism as follows in his 25 July 1985 letter: "In terms of the larger issue of

modernism, my interest stems from the fact that in one of his Liberty Hall speeches Garvey directs a cautionary word at his opponents and informs them that he can't be tampered with because, as he says, 'I am a *modern*.' That intrigued me greatly. What did he mean by that? What, in fact, did it mean in the context of the early 1920s for someone to lay claim to being 'a modern'?" I shared my own ideas on the matter with Professor Hill whose agreement seemed implicit in his notion that only an exploration of "folk types" and iconographies (e.g., Garvey as Anancy, a trickster in competition with Washington as Brer Rabbit, a trickster of a different sort) could reveal the nature of the black modern to us. Professor Hill is the editor of the Garvey papers.

66. For a definition of "carnivalesque discourse" (a term that derives from Bakhtin and that is elaborated by Julia Kristeva) and "zero-degree writing" (Roland Barthes's concept), see my discussion of *Black Boy* in *Blues, Ideology, and Afro-American Literature*.

67. *Narrative of the Life of Frederick Douglass*, ed. Houston Baker (New York: Penguin, 1982), p. 150.

68. *The Autobiography of W. E. B. DuBois*, ed. Herbert Aptheker (New York: International, 1968), p. 229.

69. Quoted from an interview I conducted with the poet on 14 October 1985. The context of the utterance was, specifically, the empowerment of black women who must resist any form of "abuse" from their own men or from the "other world."

70. Don L. Lee, *Don't Cry, Scream* (Detroit: Broadside, 1969), p. 30.

71. Hughes writes as follows in "The Twenties: Harlem and Its Negritude": "From McKay and [James Weldon] Johnson to Richard Wright and Ellison ran the Renaissance connections, with various plugs, switches, and cutoffs between. But the voltage in one way or another came through to all of us." The essay is reprinted in *Langston Hughes Review* 4 (1985): 29–36. Hughes indicates in the essay, which originally appeared in 1966, that the energies of Harlem transcended their American boundaries and carried effective voltage to the Caribbean, Africa and South Africa.

Index

Italic page numbers refer to illustrations.

Absalom, Absalom! (Faulkner), 68

Adams, Robert Martin, 1–2

Aesthetics, Kantian, 8, 110

Alger, Horatio, 31

Allaesthetic character, 49–50

"Ancestral arts" in *The New Negro*, 73

Anglo-American and Irish modernism, xv–xviii, 3–4, 13–14

Aptheker, Herbert, 76

Arnold (*Different Strokes*), 24

Arnold, Matthew, 2

Art: African, in *The New Negro*, 73; as means of advancement, 11; Western white bourgeois, xix, 106, 110

Art and Imagination of W. E. B. DuBois (Rampersad), 113n.46

Assimilationism, 12

Atlanta Exposition Address (Washington), 15, 31, 32

Atlanta University, 103

Atlantic Monthly, 43

Auden, W. H., 109n.13

Aunt Peggy (*The Conjure Woman*), 46

Authenticity, 100, 102; of voice (*see* Sound/sounding: authentic Afro-American)

Authoritarianism, 5

"Autobiographical Acts and the Voice of the Southern Slave" (Baker), 113n.43

Awkward, Michael, 114n.60

Badness, and deformation of mastery, 50

Baker, Charlotte Pierce, *105*

Baker, Eleanor Jones, 114n.62

Baker, Houston A., Jr., *105*, 113n.43

Baker, Houston A., Sr., xvi–xvii, 100–103, *105*

Baker, William and John, *105*

Bakhtin, Mikhail, 115n.66

Baldwin, James, xv, 52, 61

Baraka, Amiri, 15

Barbecue Bob, 92

Barthes, Roland, 115n.66

Benston, Kimberly, 66, 113n.51

Bercovitch, Sacvan, 71

Bergson, Henri-Louis, 3

Big Sea, The (Hughes), 110–111n.17

Bilbo, Theodore, 75

Black Boy (Wright), 81, 100

Blassingame, John, xviii

Blues, 92–95; geographics, 106

Book of American Negro Poetry, The (ed. Johnson), 38

Bookooing, 69, 114n.54

Brackenridge, Hugh Henry, 22

Bradshaw, Reverend (*A Different Drummer*), 19–20, 40

Braithwaite, Edward, 114n.61

Brancusi, Constantin, 3

Broonzy, Big Bill, 92

Brown, Sterling, 72, 92–95, 100, 114n.62

"Brown Madonna" (Reiss), 73, 80

Buchanan, Tom (*The Great Gatsby*), 4, 5, 75

Caliban (*The Tempest*), 52–54, 60, 61; tripling of, 55
Careerism, xix
Carnegie, Andrew, 31–33
Césaire, Aimé, 61
"Changing same," 14, 15, 106
"Chapel of melody," 65
Chenweizu, 7
Chesnutt, Charles Waddell, 37–38, 41–47
Chicken-stealing, 27, 33
"Civilization," Western white bourgeois, xix, 5, 6
Clemens, Samuel, 24
Cohen, Octavus Roy, 75
Confinement, xix, 110n.14
Conjure, 43–44, 46–47
"Conjurer's Revenge, The" (Chesnutt), 46
Conjure Woman, The (Chesnutt), 41, 43–47
Conrad, Joseph, 6
Continental modernism, xviii, 3
Cooper, James Fenimore, 22
Cott, H. B., 49–51
Cox, Ida, 92
Cryptic mask, 51
Cubism, 5
Cuff (*Modern Chivalry*), 22
Cullen, Countee, xvi, 10, 73, 85, 86
Cullen, Rev. Frederick, 86
Cultural performance, 58, 63–65, 67, 73–74
Culture: in DuBois, 64–65; popular, 110n.14 (*see also* Folk culture; Folklore)

Dada, white, 22. *See also* Nonsense
Day, Morris, 50
Deformation, 107; and folk sound, 93; gorilla, 51; of mastery, xviii, 49–51, 56, 67, 103–4; through radical marronage, 75; in *Up from Slavery*, 99; and the validation of folk culture, 92
Denigration of form, 85–86, 114n.60
Derrida, Jacques, 56

Dialect, 42, 44; as mask, 111n.22; poetry in, 38
Difference, in *The Tempest*, 54, 55
Different Drummer, A (Kelley), 19–20
"Dis and Dat: Dialect and the Descent" (Gates), 111n.22
Discourse: carnivalesque, 115n.66; slave-world, 101
Display: and black authorship, 56; by gorillas, 50–51, 61, 103; phaneric, 85, 103; sounds of, 55
District of Columbia, 29
"Don't Cry, Scream" (Madhubuti), 104
Doolittle, Hilda ("H. D."), 3
Douglas, Aaron, 73
Douglass, Frederick, 102, 103
DuBois, W. E. B., 37, 49, 51–52, 57–68, 88–89, 99–104
Dunbar, Paul Laurence, 8, 37–41, 49, 68–69
Durham (North Carolina), 83, 84

Einstein, Albert, 3
Eliot, T. S., xv, 3–4, 6, 87
Elitism, 4–5
Ellipsis, 16
Ellison, Ralph, xv, 27–28, 106, 111n.29, 115n.71
Emerson, Ralph Waldo, 54
Emperor Jones, The (O'Neill), 7
Equiano, Olaudah, 51
Estes, Sleepy John, 92
Exegesis, 72
Expressionism, 5

"Failure,", 9, 106
Family history, 105–6
Faulkner, William, 24
Fauset, Arthur Huff, 73
Fisk Jubilee Singers, 66–67, 67
Fisk University, 58, 64, 65
Fitzgerald, F. Scott, 4, 5, 6
Folk culture, Afro-American, 92
Folklore, Afro-American, 41, 73
Form, 16–17, 44, 47, 107; denigration of, 85–86, 114n.60; mastery

of (*see* Mastery of form); natural, 49, 54 (*see also* Display); standard, in *The New Negro*, 85–86; under renaissancism, 91–92. *See also* Deformation
Foucault, Michel, 110n.14
Frazier, E. Franklin, 83
Frazier, Sir James, 3
Freud, Sigmund, 3
Fuller, Blind Boy, 92
Futurism, 5

Gabbin, Joanne V., 114n.62
Garvey, Marcus, 81, 95–96, 98, 115n.65
Gates, Henry Louis, 111n.22
Gorilla display, 50–51, 61, 103
Gospel of Wealth (Carnegie), 31
Graphic presence, African, in *The New Negro*, 73
Graphics of minstrelsy, 41
"Gray Wolf's Ha'nt, The" (Chesnutt), 45–47
Great Gatsby, The (Fitzgerald), 4, 24
Gregory, Montgomery, 87
Groves, Colin, 50–51
Guerrilla warfare, 77

H.D., 3
Hampton-Tuskegee, 84
"Hampton-Tuskegee: Missioners of The Mass" (Moton), 84
Harlem, 74–75, 83, 84, 89, 96, 106, 115n.71; 1935 riot in, 12
Harlem Renaissance, xvii–xix, 8, 86, 91, 106–7; alleged "failure" of, xv–xvi, 9–14; Hughes on, 110–111n.17
Harlem Renaissance (Huggins), 10
Harris, Joel Chandler, 41
Hassan, Ihab, 2
Hegel, Wilhelm Friedrich, 63
Heisenberg, Werner, 3
Henderson, Stephen, 93
Henley, William Ernest, 39
Hermeneutics, 72
Hill, Robert, 95, 114–15n.65

Howard University, 84
"Howard: The National Negro University" (Miller), 84
Huckleberry Finn (Twain), 24
Huggins, Nathan, xvi, 10, 12
Hughes, Langston, xvi, 10, 106, 110–111n.17, 115n.71
Hunter, Alberta, 92
Hurston, Zora Neale, 95, 106

Imagism, 5, 87
Impressionism, 5
Insurgency, 81. *See also* Subversion
Interpretation, 72
Invictus (Henley), 39
Invisible Man (Ellison), 27–28, 56, 111n.29

Jahn, Janheinz, 113n.43
Jazz, 92
Jefferson, George (*The Jeffersons*), 24
Johnson, Charles S., 84
Johnson, James Weldon, 9, 12, 38, 115n.71
Johnson, Robert, 92
Josie ("Of the Meaning of Progress"), 64, 65
Joyce, James, xv, 3
Julius (*The Conjure Woman*), 41, 45–47
Jung, Carl, 3
"Jungle Love" as deformation of mastery, 50

Kandinsky, Wassily, 3
Kant, Immanuel, 63
Kantian aesthetics, 8, 110
Kelley, William Melvin, 19–20, 52
Kellogg, Paul, 84
Kersands, Billy, 33, 34, 111–12n.30
King Kong (*King Kong*), 52
Klee, Paul, 3
Kristeva, Julia, 115n.66
Ku Klux Klan, 62

Lamming, George, 52, 55, 113n.43
Language: Caliban's, given by

Language (*continued*)
  Prospero, 55; and tyranny, 54. *See also* Discourse
Lawrence, D. H., 6
Lee, Don L., 104
"Let Us Cheer the Weary Traveller," 58, 59
Levin, Harry, 1
Lewis, Cugo, 87
Lewis, David Levering, 10–12
Liston, Carolyn, 114n.59
"Literature," xix, 8, 100, 106
Locke, Alain, xvi, 10, 72–73, 75, 79–81, 83, 86, 87, *88*
Logan, Rayford, 98
Logocracy, 71
Lynching, 19–21, 75, 76

Madhubuti, Haki, 104
Madness and Civilization (Foucault), xix, 8, 110n.14
Ma Rainey (Brown), 93–95
Maroon Societies (Price), 76–77
Marronage, 76–79, 95, 100, 103; radical, 75; self-in-, 92, 114n.61
"Mars Jeems's Nightmare" (Chesnutt), 46
Marx, Karl, 3, 63
Masks, 17, 47; African, 57, 58, 68, 73, 95; biological, 50; and dialect, 111n.22; in Dunbar, 39; manipulation of, 25; minstrel, 17, 18, 102; in *The New Negro*, 85–86; phaneric versus cryptic, 51; sounds from (*see* Sound/Sounding)
Mason, Mrs. R. Osgood, 110n.17
Mass image, 95
Masses, Afro-American, 69, 77, 81
Mastery, deformation of. *See* Deformation: of mastery
Mastery of form, xviii, 8, 22, 31–32, 47, 50, 67, 85–87, 93
McKay, Claude, xvi, 10, 73, 85, 106, 115n.71
Migration from the South, 75, 76
Miller, Kelly, 84, 87

Minstrel mask, 17, 18, 102
Minstrelsy, 17–24, 40–41, 56, 71, 111–12n.30; graphics of, 41; sounds of (*see* Sound/Sounding)
Modern Chivalry (Brackenridge), 22
Modernism, xv–xvi, xvii–xviii, 1–8; Afro-American, 12, 93, 101; Anglo-American and Irish, xv–xviii, 3–4, 13–14; Continental, xviii, 3; Marcus Garvey's, 96
Mojo, 47
Moton, Robert R., 84
Mr. T. (*The A Team*), 24, 52
Music, 60, 65–68

Naming, 25, 99
Nationhood, Afro-American, 10, 29, 71–77, 87; and race, 79–81
Nature (Emerson), 54
"Negro Librarian, The" (Reiss), 73
"Negro Mind Reaches Out, The" (DuBois), 88–89
"Negro Pioneers" (Kellogg), 84
"Negro Teachers" (Reiss), 73
"New Frontage on American Life" (Johnson), 84
New Negro, The (Locke), 10–11, 72–81, 83–86, 91, 96, 98
New Negro Thirty Years Afterward, The (Logan), 98
Nietzsche, Friedrich, 3
Nonsense, 21, 33, 46, 47, 56; Western philosophy as, 45

O'Neill, Eugene, 7
"O, rise, shine for Thy Light is a'coming," 72
"Of the Coming of John" (DuBois), 87
"Of the Meaning of Progress" (DuBois), 64, 65
"On the Modern Element in Literature" (Arnold), 2

Page, Walter Hines, 41, 43
Parole, 60

Peggy (*The Conjure Woman*), 46
Performance, cultural, 58, 63–65,
    67, 73–74
Phaneric mask, 51
Picasso, Pablo, xv, 3
Pierce, Joseph C., Sr., *105*
Pierce, Mark Frederick, *105*
Poetic image, 16
Poetic mastery, 93
Poetry, 86–87; dialect, 38
Popular culture, 110n.14
Possession, 53, 56. *See also*
    Confinement
"POSTmodernISM: A Para-
    critical Bibliography" (Hassan),
    2
Pound, Ezra, xv, 3, 6, 87
Price, Richard, 76–77
Prospero (*The Tempest*), 55, 58, 60
Proust, Marcel, 6
Pudd'nhead Wilson (Twain), 24

Rabelais, François, 1
Race and nationhood, 79–81
Radical marronage, 75
Rainey, Gertrude "Ma," 92, 93, *96*
Rampersad, Arnold, 113n.46
Reconstruction, 28–29
Redding, J. Saunders, 75
Reed, Ishmael, 69, 114n.54
Reiss, Winold, 73; portrait of
    Locke, *88*
Religion, African, 43–44
Renaissancism, 8, 91–92, 106, 107;
    and mass image, 95
Renaming, 25, 99
Rilke, Rainer Maria, 13–14
Robeson, Paul, 73
Rohlehr, Gordon, 114n.61
Root work, 44, 46
Rourke, Constance, 17–18

Sade, 50
Salem Methodist Episcopal
    Church (Harlem), 86
Sanchez, Sonia, 103
Satanstoe (Cooper), 22

"Scholarship," xix, 13
Segregation, 11
Self-determination in *The New
    Negro*, 74–75
Self-in-marronage, 92, 114n.61
Signifying, 38, 50
"Sis' Becky's Pickaninny"
    (Chesnutt), 46
Slavery, 44, 101
Smith, Bessie, 92
Smith, Elizabeth and John, *105*
Smith, Mamie, 92
"Smooth Operator" as deforma-
    tion of mastery, 50
Song, 65–68. *See also* Blues;
    Spirituals
Sontag, Susan, 5
"Sorrow Songs," 60. *See also*
    Spirituals
Souls of Black Folk, The (DuBois),
    57–68, 72, 73
Sound/sounding: of Afro-Ameri-
    can modernism, and discursive
    strategy, xviii; alien, and defor-
    mation, 51; authentic Afro-
    American, 43, 46, 51–52, 56–58,
    66, 71, 73; in DuBois, 89; folk,
    and deformation, 93; from the
    minstrel mask, 18, 22, 24, 29–30,
    32, 42, 43 (*see also* Dialect);
    mnemonic, 41; of protective dis-
    play, 55; storied, 101
South: in *The Souls of Black Folk*,
    62–63; in *Up from Slavery*,
    62–63
Southern Road (Brown), 100
Spirit, 44
Spirit house, 95
Spirituals, 57, 58, 60, 72–73, 92
Spivey, Victoria, 92
Sport of the Gods, The (Dunbar),
    68–69
Statuary, African, 73
Stewart, Susan, 21
Stoddard, Lothrop, 4, 75
Stowe, Harriet Beecher, 22–24
Stravinsky, Igor, 3

Subversion, 110n.14. *See also* Insurgency
Sumner, William Graham, 75
Surnames, changing of, 25, 99
Surrealism, xv

"T'appin" (Lewis), 87
Tempest, The (Shakespeare), 53–54
They Came in Chains (Redding), 75–76
Tolson, Melvin, xv
Toomer, Jean, xvi, 73, 87
Topsy (*Uncle Tom's Cabin*), 23
Transformation in *The Conjure Woman*, 41, 43–47
Traylor, Eleanor, 113n.49
Trickster re-forming of minstrel role, 47
Trickster tales, 41
Trilling, Lionel, 5–7
Tripling of Caliban, 55
Trope, 16
Turner, Nat, 52
Tuskegee, 30–33, 37, 62. *See also* Hampton-Tuskegee
Twain, Mark, 24
"Twenties, The" (Hughes), 115n.71

Ulysses (Joyce), xv, 3, 7, 21
Uncle Julius (*The Conjure Woman*), 41, 45–47
Uncle Tom's Cabin (Stowe), 22–24
Unrepresentable, the, 5
Up from Slavery (Washington), xviii, 16, 25–36, 40, 62–63, 68, 99, 100

Veil, 51–52 (*see also* Mask); in *The Souls of Black Folk*, 57
"Vestiges" (Brown), 100
Vodun (Voodoo), 43–44
Vorticism, 5

Walker George, 20, 33, 111–12n.30
Warburg, Aby, xx
Warren, Robert Penn, 72
Washington, Booker T., xvii, 15–16, 37, 38, 40, 41, 62, 67–68, 85, 99, 101; as southern spokesperson, 28–29
Washington (D.C.), 29, 37–38
Waste Land, The (Eliot), xv, 3, 86
"We Wear the Mask" (Dunbar), 39
West, Dorothy, 9
"West and the Rest of Us" (Chenweizu), 7
Western philosophy, 47; as nonsense, 45
"What Was Modernism?" (Levin), 1
"White House, The" (McKay), 85
Whitman, Walt, 3
Williams, Bert, 20, 33, 35, 111–12n.30
Wilson, Woodrow, 75
Woodward, C. Vahn, 75
Woolf, Virginia, 3
Work, John, 93
Wright, Richard, 81, 95, 100, 103, 106, 115n.71
Writing, 60

Yeats, William Butler, 6